ARE YOU LIBERAL? LIBERTARIAN? CONSERVATIVE? OR CONFUSED?

December 12, 2016

Joseph P. Hawranek, Ph.D.

Copyright © 2019 by Joseph P. Hawranek, Ph.D..

ISBN   978-1-970160-44-4 Ebook
ISBN   978-1-970160-45-1 Paperback

All rights reserved. No part of this publication may be reproduced, distributed, or transmitted in any form or by any means, including photocopying, recording, or other electronic or mechanical methods without the prior written permission of the publisher. For permission requests, solicit the publisher via the address below through mail or email with the subject line "Attention: Publication Permission".

EC Publishing LLC
11100 SW 93rd Court Road, Suite 10-215
Ocala, Florida 34481-5188, USA

Ordering Information:
Quantity sales. Special discounts are available on quantity purchases by corporations, associations, and others. For details, contact the publisher at the address above.

www.ecpublishingllc.com
info@ecpublishingllc.com
+1 (352) 234-6201

Printed in the United States of America

CONTENTS

PREFACE xi
   What Are the Differences Between Socialism and
   Libertarianism?... xiii
   Libertarianism xiii
   Socialism xiv
INTRODUCTION xvii
CHAPTER 1 1
DEFINITIONS OF POLITICAL TERMS 1
   Underlying Question of All Economics 1
   Evolving Philosophy Of Government 1
   Libertarianism 3
   Marx and Socialism 5
      Different Types of Socialism 5
         Economic Principles 6
         Russian Socialism 6
         Social – Democratic Socialism 7
         Conservative Socialism 8
   POLITICAL SCALES 9
CHAPTER 2 10
WHERE DO YOU FIT? 10
   ARE YOU LIBERAL? LIBERTARIAN?
   CONSERVATIVE? or CONFUSED? 10
      Definitions of Political Terms 10
         Liberal 10
         Conservative 11

  Natural Law: Juris Naturalists (Latin) - Libertarianism 11
  Natural Law and Common Law 14
  Statists 16
  Political Power 16
  Freedom and Liberty 17
  Nature of Political Power 17
  Categories of Encroachment 18
  New World Order 19
ENGLISH MERCANTILE SYSTEM 22
21ST CENTURY MERCANTILISM 24
POLITICAL SPECTRUM 27
EXHIBIT 1, ANOTHER POLITICAL SPECTRUM 28
  The Middle Ground 29
  Republicans and Democrats 29
  Republican Democracy 30
CHAPTER 3 31
IS AMERICA SOCIALIST, FASCIST, A DEMOCRATIC REPUBLIC or A NEW WORLD ORDER STATE? 31
THE "ISMS" 31
  Capitalism 31
  Welfare Statism 33
  Socialism and Communism 34
LENIN'S TEN POINT PROGRAM FOR COMMUNISM 34
 1. Abolition of property in land and application of all rents of land to public purposes 35
 2. A heavy progressive or graduated income tax 35
 3. Abolition of all right of inheritance 35
 4. Confiscation of the property of all emigrants and rebels 35
 5. Centralization of credit in the hands of the State, by means of a national bank with State capital and an exclusive monopoly 36

6. Centralization of the means of communication and transport in the hands of the State..................................36
7. Extension of factories and instruments of production owned by the State; the bringing into cultivation of waste - lands, and the improvement of the soil generally in accordance with a common plan 37
8. Equal liability (financially and legally responsible for something) of all to labor. In Establishment of industrial armies, especially for agriculture..37
9. Combination of agriculture with manufacturing industries; gradual abolition of the distinction between town and country, by a more equitable distribution of the population over the country..38
10. Free education for all children in public schools. Abolition of children's factory labor in its present form. Combination of education with industrial production 38
1. Invoke a Terrifying Internal and External Enemy........40
2. Create a Gulag...40
3. Develop a Thug Caste... 41
4. Set up An Internal Surveillance System 41
5. Harass Citizen's Groups.. 41
6. Engage In Arbitrary Detention and Release................42
7. Target Key Individuals.. 42
8. Control the Press... 42
9. Dissent Equals Treason 43
10. Suspend the Rule of Law.. 43
AN EXPANDED POLITICAL SPECTRUM...................44
EXHIBIT 2, AN EXPANDED POLITICAL SPECTRUM 45
NEW WORLD ORDER 46
   Intellectual Leadership 46
   Test for Socialism and Fascism 49
   New World Order Currency and Banking 50
   International Army.. 50
   NWO Political Structure 51

Supra National Trade Policies 51
　EXHIBIT 3, EXPANDED SPECTRUM WITH NEW
　WORLD ORDER 53
　ECONOMIC SYSTEMS 54
　PRINCIPLES OF AUSTRIAN ECONOMICS 56
　SUMMARY 60
CHAPTER 3 61
QUO VADIS? – LIBERTY, FREEDOM AND POLITICAL
　LEADERSHIP 61
　QUO VADIS? 61
　WILL AMERICA CONTINUE AS A SUPER
　POWER? 63
　AMERICA'S HISTORY OF INDIVIDUAL FREEDOM
　IN NATURAL LAW 65
　　Liberty 69
　　John Locke (Libertarian) 71
　　American Liberty Documents 72
　　The Fall of The Roman Empire 74
　　Politician vs Statesman 74
　LIBERTY IN TODAY'S WORLD 76
　　National Freedom 76
　　Economic Freedom 77
　　Spiritual Freedom 77
　　Scientific Freedom 77
　　Revolution? 78
　JOHN LOCKE AND REVOLUTION 79
　　A Government That Substitutes Arbitrary Will of The
　　Executive for Law 80
　　A Government That Limits the Legislature Power from
　　Acting Freely 80
　　A Government That Delivers the People into a Foreign
　　Power 80
　　A Government that Alters the Mode of Electing the
　　Legislative Body 81
　CONCLUSION 82

- APPENDIX A - TEST 85
    - Individual Rights 86
    - Personal Freedoms 86
    - Economic Freedoms 87
    - Government Responsibility 87
        - EXHIBIT 3, LIBERAL, LIBERTARIAN, CONSERVATIVE MEASUREMENT SCALE 89
        - Subjective Scale Measures 89
        - Libertarian Scale 91
        - TABLE 1, LIBERTARIAN PERCENTAGE CALCULATIONS 92
        - TABLE 2, PERCENT LIBERTARIAN CALCULATION RESULTS 92
- BIBLIOGRAPHY 93
- GLOSSARY 95
- About Joseph P Hawranek 103
- About Raven Publishing 105
- INDEX 107

PREFACE

Liberal

"Fascism is opposed to classical liberalism, which arose as a reaction to absolutism and exhausted its historical function when the state became the expression of the conscience and will of the people. Liberalism denied the state in the name of the individual; Fascism reasserts the rights of the state and is expressing the real essence of the individual." - Benito Mussolini, 1922-194

"The Liberal Party is one which believes that, as new conditions and problems arise beyond the power of men and women to meet as individuals, it becomes the duty of Government itself to find new remedies with which to meet them. The liberal party insists that the Government has the definite duty to use all its power and resources to meet new social problems with new social controls—to ensure to the average person the right to his own economic and political life, liberty and the pursuit of happiness." – Franklin Delano Roosevelt, 1941

Libertarian

"Libertarian socialism is properly to be regarded as the inheritor of the liberal ideals of the Enlightenment." - Noam Chomsky

Freedom is the essence of man – "the possibility of a person acting according to his own decisions and plans, in contrast to the position of one who was irrevocably subject to the will of another, by arbitrary decision could coerce them to act or not to act in specific ways." – F. A. Hayek

"Every man has a property in his own person. This nobody has any right to but himself. The labor of his body, and the work of his hands, we may say, is properly his. Whatsoever that he removes out of the state nature has provided, and left it in, he has mixed his labor with that is his own, and thereby makes it his property." – John Locke

Socialism

"Socialism means slavery." – Lord Acton

"Democracy is indispensable to socialism." – Vladimir Lenin

"The goal of socialism is communism." – Vladimir Lenin

"Democracy and socialism have nothing in common but one word, equality. But notice the difference: while democracy seeks equality in liberty, socialism seeks equality in restraint and servitude." – Alexis de Tocqueville

I decided to write this book because of the 2016 presidential campaign. I found that the ***"talking heads"*** on TV expound distortions and misinformation associated with liberalism, libertarianism, conservatism, and all the other "isms". Most are based upon ignorance. One of the factors that cause confusion is time. The meanings of the words change with time. I also discovered that some of my own beliefs were confused. Thus, I set about to try to clarify my thinking and in the process differentiate in my mind the differences between these social beliefs that have pervaded our society for a couple hundred years.

ARE YOU LIBERAL? LIBERTARIAN? CONSERVATIVE? OR CONFUSED?

What Are the Differences Between Socialism and Libertarianism?

First, I tried to understand and be very explicit in the definition of socialism and libertarianism. In the process, I read several classical books on the topics. These are documented in my references. I ended up writing a new book that should be out concurrent with this – *What Are the Differences between Socialism and Libertarianism?* Below is a brief summary of the book. It is relevant for this book as background.

Libertarianism

With respect to Libertarianism, I relied heavily on David Boaz and his outstanding book, *The Libertarian Mind*. I investigated libertarian history, and the concepts embedded in libertarianism. I found that there is no master philosopher for libertarianism. In fact, it is *a philosophy of individual freedom that goes back thousands of years and is innate in all human beings*. As a result, I reviewed libertarian beliefs and the roots of libertarianism as they exist in society and are promoted by individuals who practice the philosophy. I also reviewed the rise of the new libertarian movement. In the process, I discovered libertarian beliefs about the rights an individual should have, the dignity of the individual and their modus operandi with respect to toleration of other beliefs. Further, I reviewed the law and the Constitution in order to understand their beliefs about the constitutional limits of government. I also reviewed their beliefs about the practices of government that they believe are wrong. In particular, they do not like special interest laws, government regulations, and government by waiver and over criminalization of our society.

This led to investigating government as to why they get too large. Finally, I briefly reviewed the *"deep state"* within government. The deep state is the tens of thousands of bureaucrats within government. It is the reason why governments get too big. The bureaucrats want to keep their jobs; therefore, there is an internal bias to continual growth of their group as well as the continuation of further regulations emanating from government.

Socialism

I also reviewed socialism because in America, the two have many factors in common with Liberalism. In socialism, there is a definite source and philosopher of these concepts. I started with Karl Marx, whose book, **_Das Capital_**, provides the philosophical foundation for all socialism. Then, I looked at _Russian Socialism_ that was instituted in Russia after its revolution. It has now failed. I discovered that probaby the major difference between socialism and libertarianism is associated with private property. Is Socialism, the state is supreme whereas in Libertarianism, the individual it supreme. In Socialism, the state owns property. In Libertarianism, the individual owns property. We examine the source of the concept of property in civilization - why the concept arose, why it is important for individual freedom, why it is the foundation of the price system that works in free societies and finally, why state ownership of property is doomed to failure in theory.

After analyzing "pure socialism" or Marxism in Russia, I examined a variation of the Russian socialism that followed W WII in Germany. This German socialism is called, *"Social Democratic Socialism"*. It corrects the Russian socialism problem of State control of all private property and all means of production. The intellectuals concluded that this did not work because it had the fatal flow of no private property, no pricing system and no way to calculate profits that are used to make decisions in the capitalist system.

Germany's socialism corrected that flaw and their socialism allows ownership of property, private control of production or manufacturing and the full use of the price system to make decisions. However, the

German system still controls the individual and corporations by controlling profits. The government sets percentages by law as to what profits go to the owner, how much of the profits can be reinvested and the remainder goes to the socialist state to be distributed equitably to the people in the form of state services. This type of socialism is being used in Germany and other nations in Europe. They call this distribution and sharing of profits from manufacturing operation not owned or managed by the people – *"equal opportunity"*.

In America, the Democratic Party appears to have accepted this type of socialism. Bernie Sanders wants government control of virtually everything but wants taxes based on profits to pay for it. The individual should enjoy the benefits of private production and profits by taxing the profits and redistributing them. This is close to German socialism that exists today. I note that Bernie does not promote control of production rather *"equal opportunity"* of profit sharing.

Finally, I investigated what is called - *"Socialism of Conservatism"*. Conservatism implies that the participants want no change but will only accept incremental change. This form of socialism is prevalent in France and Italy. It attempts to preserve the "rights" of the old aristocracy by slowing change. It uses the tools of "Price Controls" (supply side) and *"Behavior Control"* (demand side). This is a feudal system concept. *"Go to the Lord of the Manor to get permission to make changes."* This type of socialism is not prevalent in America because we do not have a history of feudalism practices.

I found it useful to create a spreadsheet on the different forms of socialism. The concepts become confusing if not differentiated clearly. I used the same categories across all three forms of socialism. There were (1) Means of production, (2) Capital formation, (3) Motivation. (4) Differences between socialism practice and capitalism in the power to control production.

The conclusion was that socialism in theory would fail. It has the fatal flaw of state control of production and the associated private property without the freedom of owners making decisions based on prices and profits. The German system tries to correct that flaw but they do not have the resources to carry the social programs of all the nations in the EU nor do the people of Germany want to carry that load. In practice, Marxist socialism has failed in Russia. In Europe, it is in the process of failing with the governments running out of money to finance all the social services that the politicians have promised. The people of Germany do not want to shoulder that load even though the political leaders and their banker financial backers want to continue the move toward European regionalization and New World Order global government direction. The European Union is failing as countries start to leave because of socialism's failure to provide services. The UK has left and I expect Italy to be next. The bankers "austerity" programs are not acceptable to the people who have been used to and adjusted to free services from government. The coming financial collapse due to the massive non-payable debt will cause all the people and their associated nations to come to grips with what they want to give their children – austerity or prosperity. The latter comes from capitalism, private property and a free society. The former comes from a centrally controlled social system that removes either private property or private profits from society and substitutes a centralized bureaucracy that makes the decisions for all government and all the people in Europe.

INTRODUCTION

I originally thought that it would be reasonable to put a book together that had the economic theory of socialism and libertarianism along with the challenge of asking the question of *"Are You Liberal, Libertarian, Conservative or Confused?"* Upon completing the first part, I realized that I had a stand-alone book that was detailed, factual, and that clearly shows the differences in in the philosophy of the movements. I called it, *What Are the Differences Between Socialism and Libertarianism?* It should be interesting to readers of this book. It describes what has been happening with those two philosophies of government. It serves as a sound foundation for this book. However, I kept it separate from this book because I was having fun trying to create a scale that covered the diverse topics of this book. I did not want to defocus the reader from him finding out where he stood on these scales.

I wrote the first book to document differences between the movements. I did not want to detract from the big question of this book, *"Are You Liberal, Libertarian, Conservative or Confused?"*, so I made the first half of my research into a standalone eBook that is available on my website, www.ravengeopolnews.com.

That book provides definitions of liberal / socialist, libertarian and conservative philosophies of government. However, for this book, only a summary of the results is required. Accordingly, I am including them as background of this book. This material is found in Chapter 1, Background.

My approach in this book is to apply a scale to the philosophical positions of belief that exist in our society. At best, these are estimates but still useful in thinking about yourself. I started with Richard Maybury's book, ***Are You Liberal, Conservative or Confused?***. It was an inspiration and clear but it was published in 1993. I tried to update it by adding Libertarian to the scales. Further, my analysis found socialism in the US and liberalism as overlapping philosophies. They follow the same objectives. In my book, ***What Are the Differences Between Socialism and Libertarianism?***, I discussed in detail the differences between socialism and libertarianism. The modern American liberal has moved philosophically closer to the European model of socialism.

In Chapter 2 – Are You Liberal, Conservative, Libertarian or Confused? I provide definitions and create linear scales. I also provide a questionnaire test that the reader can use to determine where he fits on the three dimensional scale. The reader is challenged to take the short test twice. First, before you read the book and the second time after you finish the book. The test is available in Appendix A, TEST WHETHER YOU ARE LIBERAL, LIBERTARIAN, CONSERVATIVE OR CONFUSED. As I developed the scaling, I increased the complexity of the scales from Exhibit to Exhibit so that the reader can easily follow and place their beliefs somewhere on the scale.

In Chapter 3 - Is America Socialist, Fascist, A Democratic Republic or A New World Order State? I directly address the problem facing the citizen in a constantly changing world with constant propaganda coming from the New World Order advocates. I explain what they envision by showing their stated objectives, which are oriented to a world government with a few "chosen ones" running the world.

In Chapter 4, Quo Vadis? – Liberty, Freedom and Political Leadership, I note that America is at a Cross Roads. I agree with Donald Trump, we need to *"drain the swamp"* in DC, put new people in place and resume living by the constitution.

Chapter 5 – Conclusions, summarizes the results of the analysis.

My approach to the research required for this book was to go to experts, read their material and summarize it for you. Of course, I used judgment in the choice of material and the documentation of what I felt important. I also added my beliefs from studying this field for many years. Nonetheless, I feel that I have stood on the shoulders of giants. The men that I used as my sources were outstanding in their fields and clear in their thinking. I extend the thinking into the future and see what it means to America.

I concluded the America is fundamentally Libertarian and has been since its founding. However, the elitist politicians are not – they are liberal / progressive/socialist. This is one of the reasons that the Democratic elite were so shocked at Trump being elected over Clinton. The Elite were hard driving their views of Liberal / Socialism into this nation. The voters rejected them. Today, the Democrats are focusing on the mechanics of why Clinton lost – not the philosophies proposed that were rejected. They still believe them to be true. The voters rejected them because they are more libertarian than socialist and do not want a centrist, socialist government. It will take a while and a change of leadership before the Democratic Party wakes up.

I found that the Liberal / Progressives (two names for the same movement) made major inroads into the mores of America during the 20th Century. In this 21st Century, the revolt of the new generation is that they find that the government is doing too much, doing it poorly, becoming too constraining, taking too much of their money and negatively affecting all segments of society from birth to death. This approach to government is being rejected in the UK – Brexit and in the US – Donald Trump winning over all odds.

CHAPTER 1
DEFINITIONS OF POLITICAL TERMS

Underlying Question of All Economics

I use the definition that Economics is the study of man in his everyday life. *What is the best way to organize society that maximizes the wealth of the nation and the individual?* The answer is a matter of opinion. Some say they want centralized control of the state so that our bureaucrats in DC can *"fairly"* distribute the wealth. Alternatively, others say that they created the wealth and they do not want DC to distribute it to anyone. They should have the right to the wealth that they created with their own labor.

Evolving Philosophy Of Government

The history of the 20th century has shown that the centrist philosophers represented by Marx socialism and Mussolini / Hitler fascism and John Maynard Keynes in the US has failed. They failed because nation states that accepted and implemented those philosophies now understand that Margaret Thatcher was right, *"Socialism works great until you run out of other peoples' money."* In the US, we have found that bigger government generally benefits the government bureaucrats, the corporations standing behind the politicians and the politicians but not the citizens.

During the 20th century, America was led by Liberal politicians that believe in the centralized control of just about everything. The country has deteriorated greatly from this approach and has a national debt of $20 trillion that arguably cannot be repaid and this proves the point. The debt went from $9 trillion to $20 trillion during the Obama administration.

America is at a Cross Roads. Does it want to become a Democratic Socialist society or be a Republican Democratic free enterprise Capitalist society? The way society is organized can be Centrist of Distributed. The Centrist society is Socialist and Fascist. The Republican Democratic free enterprise Capitalist society is distributed. Clearly, a vote for Hillary Clinton gives one the Centrist Socialist society. A vote for Donald Trump gives the nation a Republican Democratic free enterprise Capitalist society.

For the last 100 years, the Progressives who came to power about 1900 evolved their name from Progressives to Liberal and are now evolving their movement name to Socialist. I find it interesting that the modern Liberal /Progressive do not like to be called socialist. Recall that the Liberal of the 1800s was a modern day Libertarian. All the founding fathers were Libertarian. In addition, man's basic instincts are Libertarian.

This evolution of definitions and chameleon like changes from era to era can causeconfusion in anyone's mind. A Progressive of 1910 became what is now called Liberal. However, the modern Liberal /Progressive are now evolving into a Socialist – even though they do not like to think of themselves as socialists. Upon investigation, one finds that there are different types of socialists, which will be covered later in this chapter.

Finally, I have found that writers and commentators in articles at times misuse terms. In this book, I attempt to clarify and discretely define terms so that their use would be less confusing. Further, I put definitions in italics. The subject matter is complex and one needs to refer back at times in order to keep the differences distinct in your mind.

The liberal / socialist believe that the state has the right to make regulations from the central government for all of us. The fact that many of these rulings are in direct conflict with the written constitution is glossed over with platitudes like *"the constitution is a fluid document"*. Further, they believe that government is all-powerful over the individual and that immoral acts such as abortion and same sex marriage are valid because the state says so and the state overrides religious morality held by 90% of the Christians in the nation. This is a clear instance where the state overrides God's teachings.

Libertarianism

In the 19th century, a Liberal was what we would call a Libertarian today. At the beginning of the 20th century, the philosophy and concept of liberal thinking was attacked by bankers such as J.P. Morgan and Paul Warburg. At the time, Liberals were libertarians and they made decisions using reason. J.P. Morgan had a famous quote, *"I don't want thinkers. I want workers."* Accordingly, he went about changing the education system in America. How he did it and who he chose to do it is covered in my book, *Who's Next?*

These men endorsed progressive education and backed progressives in politics. I believe that these men met in secret and planned how to take control of United States. They met at Jekyll Island in 1910. This is well documented in Ed Griffin's book, *The Creature from Jekyll Island* and in my book, *Who's Next? Analysis Of Fed Plundering In*

Port Usury (New York). How Much Booty Is It? Mr. Griffin focused on the Federal Reserve and my book extended that focus to theft by Federal Reserve Banks, education and senatorial politics.

The bankers were successful. The 20th century in America is one of movement toward centrist government and progressivism with the individual and libertarians being hobbled by laws and government regulations. It is only recently that libertarianism has been making a comeback. The reason for the comeback is simple. Progressive liberalism as practiced by a centrist government under a philosophy such as socialism has failed in multiple countries in Europe. The Keynes form of Centralized control of government has also failed. The EU economies are failing, their debt is unpayable and unemployment is soaring. This results in the citizen being less well off than he was 50 to 75 years ago.

Libertarians are saying that socialism, liberalism and fascism, all of which were tried in the 20th century, have failed and it is time to get back to libertarianism, which grew this nation from 1776 to 1913 to be one of the greatest nations on earth. Libertarians focus on the individual and the dignity of the individual. They specify very clearly what rights an individual should have. They believe that these rights come from God not the state. However, they recognize that some society has many different types of people creating a diverse society. This pluralism means that individuals must learn to be and become tolerant.

Libertarians believe in the law. They understand that there can be no freedom unless there is law and it is enforced. Accordingly, they firmly believe in Constitutional limits on government. Finally, they disagree with government special interest laws that provide benefits to special interests at the expense of the citizen. One example is that they do not believe in government by waiver. This means that the president as the executive does not have the right to allow certain states to bow out of belonging to or participating in the law such as was done with the Affordable Care Act known as Obama Care. That would be legislation by the Executive rather than enforcement.

In summary, Libertarians presume that all men are free. In the presumption of liberty and personal freedom, *p*eople ought to be free to live as they choose unless advocates of coercion can make a compelling case

Marx and Socialism

Communism puts an end to the division of life into public and private spheres. It gives the state control over individuals and subsumes those individuals to always believe the common good is better than individual freedom of choice. I note that Communism is Godless for a purpose. Socialism uses Communism to eliminate God. They need to do this because they are substituting the "state" for "God" as the authority. This nullifies thousands of years of tradition and law. Further, it goes against Natural law, which to them does not exist because it conflicts with what the state may want to do. This is analogous to the emperors and kings in Europe who refused to acknowledge natural law because it conflicted with their dictates. This is not the American way nor is it the way of English speaking people all over the earth.

Different Types of Socialism

Here are some general conclusions we can make.

Socialism has a number of forms and to understand the difference, we need to discuss

- Economic Principles
- Russian socialism
- Social – Democratic socialismas in Germany and Europe

- Conservative Socialism

Economic Principles

All society has two fundamental economic principles, which are scarcity and property. From these two concepts, other definitions flow.

- *Aggression* is aggression against property.
- *Contract* defines a nonaggressive relationship between property owners.
- *Socialism* is an institutionalized policy of aggression against property by the state.
- *Capitalism* is an institutionalized recognition of individual property rights and contracts.

A person digging a well in the desert creates *property* from *scarcity*. He is a *capitalist*. The state using force to make the owner provide water to everyone without compensation is *socialism*.

Russian Socialism

During the Russian revolution, the revolutionaries established a full implementation of Marxism that is characterized by the state ownership of all means of production, no private property and no God. It is inherently defective since pricing is not used to determine what should be produced, what equipment to use, how much should be produced and what price should be charged. It is doomed to fail since no centralized government system can optimally make all those decisions. Only a privately held property owner can optimize the constantly changing environment. He must make decisions based on price and cost and how it affects his profits.

The Russian system requires production overseers that are chosen politically not meritocratically. Therefore, individuals optimize their political skills and not their production skills since that is what is rewarded.

Social – Democratic Socialism

This is the name for the German Republic economic system. The Germans watched Russia's socialism fail. They understood the Marxian socialism and decided not to use it because factors of production ownership by the government is fundamentally flawed and doomed to failure. As a result, the German system allows private ownership and private control of production, which eliminates the Russian problem. However, the government controls the earnings via legislation and taxes. The state determines how much of the earnings go into new capital production as well as dividends and taxes for the non-producing and non-owning members of the state.

A comparison between capitalism and the German social democratic socialism show that -

- In capitalism, the owner makes the decision to produce, which equipment to buy, which production to run and which investment to make and how to distribute profits. The owner is in control.

- In social democratic socialism, the owner makes all the decision to produce and which equipment to buy; but the state determines how much of the profits should go into investment, how much profit goes to the owner and the rest goes to the state and the citizens. The state enters into the control.

Conservative Socialism

This is similar to Germany's socialism but adds the aristocratic nobility in the nation as influence agents. They influence the parliament to keep changes from being too rapid. They are trying to maintain the old capitalist system. To accomplish this, they use price control on products (the supply side) and behavior controls (the demand side) on purchasing decisions.

The general conclusions of this analysis on socialism are –

- In socialism, the natural owners of property are partially or totally expropriated to the advantage of nonusers, non-contractors and non-producers.

- Russia proved that state ownership of all factors of production in a socialistic society, per Marx's philosophy, fails.

- The goal of socialism is the abolition of capitalism as a social system.

- The current goal of socialism is to provide equal opportunity for all citizens. However, opportunity means in this instance equal sharing of profits from the factors of production. It is not opportunity to earn those profits in meritocratic ways as it is in America.

- In Germany, for large corporations, the state determines how profits are distributed. They determine how much is to be reinvested, how much is to go to the owners and how much is to remain in the state for its citizens. They do this with legislation and taxation.

- Conservative socialism is a name provided for those instances where the nobility is still not forgotten. It is conservative since it is trying to maintain the old capitalist system. It uses the methods of price controls and behavior controls to slow the process of a march towards a socialistic society.

I think it is fair to say that in Europe today, their problems stem from their socialistic practices. There is not enough money for all the services that politicians legislate for the citizens. They legislate these services in order to be reelected. However, Margaret Thatcher said it best, *"Socialism is great until you run out of other people's money."*

POLITICAL SCALES

First, we start on a linear scale from Left (Liberal) to Right (Conservative). On that scale are placed all of the political groups such as communist, fascist, socialist and so on. From there we add more complexity and introduce the New World Order. Finally, we introduce a very detailed political spectrum showing the New World Order with all the other political delineations. The concepts are layered to make it easier to understand.

The final circular scale shows most of the entities that exist in America today. It raises the question, Quo Vadis? Where do we go from here? Do we become a socialized state as in Europe and follow the path that we know will lead to failure? Alternatively, do we let America grow free and expand in a capitalist system again to reach greatness based on its physical and people resources. The latter requires more work since the role of the state is minimal. To do the later will require that we get back to our roots and allow free enterprise to flourish within the constraints of our Constitution.

In Conclusion, America stands at a crossroads. Do we want socialism and centralized governmental control of our lives, which is the next step toward the totalitarian state that the New World Order centrists want? Alternatively, do we want to go back to a nation of individual liberty and freedom that Libertarians represent? Our choice of directions is clear in the 2016 election – vote Hillary Clinton for centrist socialist state. Vote Donald Trump for individual freedom

CHAPTER 2

WHERE DO YOU FIT?

ARE YOU LIBERAL?LIBERTARIAN?CONSERVATIVE? or CONFUSED?

Definitions of Political Terms

The terms to be discussed in this paper are defined as "soft" because their meaning varies with time and are understood to be relative to one another. Therefore, it is necessary to define basic terms as concretely as possible prior to discussing them in relationship with one another. Let us begin with some definitions that are used here.

Liberal

The Columbia encyclopedia saying that *"liberalism is based, in general, on faith in progress and the ability and goodness of man, and on the firm belief in the importance of the rights and welfare of the individual".* Webster's Unabridged Dictionary says liberals favor *"political reforms tending toward democracy and freedom for the individual".* Thus, *liberals advocate steady change, consideration of the individual and progress.*

Conservative

The Columbia encyclopedia says that conservatism is *"the desire to maintain, or conserve, the existing order"*. Webster's Unabridged Dictionary says conservatives *"tend to conserve old institutions, methods and customs."* Thus, *conservatives value the wisdom of the past and are generally opposed to widespread reform unless it demonstrates an improvement for the citizen over the past.*

Natural Law: Juris Naturalists (Latin) - Libertarianism

Natural Law was the belief held by the founding fathers of this nation. They based their beliefs on the philosophy of John Locke (the first Libertarian). It is also the belief of many Americans today.

Many of the founders were intellectuals who read the classics in their original Greek and Latin. They knew that Socrates introduced the concept of *"the perfect good"* or God. Emperor Augustus, the stoic, introduced Socrates's concept of one supreme God (Jupiter) into Roman law. Augustus made the belief in one God part of the mandatory Roman state religion. Next, the early Christian Paul, also a well-educated intellectual and a stoic, used the Roman concept of one God and identified him as being Jesus of Nazareth in his teachings. This was a major change from the mythical to the real – Jesus had just been killed. Finally, the Church fathers of Augustine and Thomas Aquinas solidified Paul's teachings into Christian religious doctrines. Those early Catholic religious doctrines provided the founding doctrines of all protestant faiths including the Anglican Church. I note that most if not all of the founders were Anglican Protestants in their beliefs and practices. It is a matter of record that the founders of this Nation were all Christian believers, read and understood multiple languages, were well read in the classics and were knowledgeable in Christian theology and thus Natural Law. The founders believed that Natural Law and man's law had a structure wherein Natural Law was higher than man's law. This was a common European belief since the time of Sophocles in Greece (Zeus) and Cicero in Rome (Jupiter) and Augustus in Rome (Jesus) who believed in a God of natural law who superseded black letter law.

It was Emperor Constantine who changed the use of Jupiter as God to use Jesus as God in the 4thcentury. Augustus followed Constantine. This common belief among all the founders was also common among the American population who, at the time, were primarily of English Anglican heritage or other protestant denominations. What follows are some quotes that state the Colonial beliefs of the times. It should be noted that Natural Law is the greatest contribution of Greece and Rome to the U.S. Cicero was the first person to define Natural Law that was actually incorporated into the Roman constitution. God for the Romans was a monotheist Jupiter

> *"True law is right reason in agreement with nature, derived from God, universal, consistent, everlasting, whose nature is to advocate duty by prescription and deter wrong doing by prohibition. Good men obey this prescription, but evil men disobey them. It is forbidden by God to alter this law, nor is it permissible to repeal any part of it, and it is impossible to abolish the whole of it. Neither the Senate nor the People can absolve us from obeying this law and we do not need to look outside ourselves for an expounder or interpreter of this law. There will not be one law for Rome and another law for Athens. There is now and will be forever one law, valid for all people and all times, And, there will be one master and ruler for all of us in common, God, who is the author of this law, its promulgator, and enforcing judge. Whoever does not obey this law is trying to escape himself and deny his nature as a human being. By this very fact, he will suffer the greatest penalties, even if he should somehow escape conventional punishments." - - - Cicero (106 BC – 43 BC)*

> "...All men are created equal, that they are endowed by their Creator with certain unalienable rights" - - Declaration of Independence, Thomas Jefferson, 1776.

> "The natural rights of the colonists are these: first, a right to life; second to liberty; third, to property; together with the right to defend them in the best manner they can." - - Samuel Adams, 1772

> "I believe there is one supreme most perfect being. I believe He is pleased and delights in the happiness of those He has created; and since without virtue man can have no happiness in this world, I firmly believe He delights to see me virtuous." - - Benjamin Franklin, "Articles of Belief and Acts of Religion" (1728)

> "It cannot be emphasized too strongly or too often that this great nation was founded, not by religionists, but by Christians; not on religions, but on the gospel of Jesus Christ! For this very reason peoples of other faiths have been afforded asylum, prosperity, and freedom of worship here." - - Patrick Henry

Thomas Jefferson, John Adams, James Madison, Ben Franklin, Patrick Henry and most of the other founding fathers were *"classical liberals"*. They were Juris Naturalists. A current popular name for their beliefs is *"Libertarianism"*. Juris Naturalists desire to minimize government and obey higher Natural Law. They understand that God gave them the means of reason and that it was their responsibility to use reason to determine the Natural Law of God. This is called Natural Law and whatever that reasoned law was – it superseded man's law.

All the founders had a common sense of "virtue" that was mentioned by Ben Franklin. In this period, virtue was considered very important and it was taught in schools. Virtue referred to a general moral goodness, which meant to them both the *Christian theological virtues* of *faith*, hope and *charity;* and the *Cardinal virtues of Greece and Rome* of *prudence, justice, temperance* and *fortitude (courage)*. The Moral Law of the Christian founders had two sets of laws or codes by which they lived their lives and thesewere both found in the Bible. The first code of Law was the *10 commandments of the Old Testament* and the second was the New Testament Law of Jesus who preached his laws of love in his Sermon on the Mount. In the New Testament, Jesus proclaimed that the two greatest commandments are **to *"love the Lord thy God with all thy heart"*** and to ***"love thy neighbor as thyself,"*** and that ***"on these two commandments hang all the law and the prophets."*** The Apostle James spoke of Christ's gospel as ***"the perfect law of liberty."*** (James 1:25).

Natural Law and Common Law

Natural Law was understood to be the set of rules that govern the operation of the universe and everyone and everything in it. Sir Isaac Newton described this very well in his writings. His job, as he saw it, was to discover God's laws of the universe so that mankind could use them. These laws existed but were unknown to man until man discovered them by use of the reasoning that God gave man.

The founding fathers believed that natural law was universal and was God's law given to man. God gave man the faculty of reason and common sense to understand the law. Common sense was understood to consist of what people in common would agree upon. Specifically, that which they **"<u>sense</u>"** as their common natural understanding is common sense. Some people use the phrase to refer to <u>beliefs</u> or <u>propositions</u> that most people would consider <u>prudent</u> and of sound <u>judgment</u>. Thus, *a reasonable meaning to the phrase is having good sense and sound judgment in practical matters.*

The founders believed that Natural Law was above man's law. The moral compass that the founders used was Christianity and its doctrines. These men were all statesmen in the sense that they had a *moral compass*, a *vision*, a set of *principles of individual freedom* and the *ability to communicate* and convince others of their visionary ideas. Very few politicians have this set of virtues and the ones that do are called statesmen.

The founders were firm on having a Nation under Common law rather than Roman law. Why? Roman law was based on a constitution but one man – the emperor - at the top could overrule the law. The emperor could decree whatever he liked over the natural law of what was right and his ruling became the de-facto law. Common Law is the system of applying and determining Natural Law that governs humans. It is the body of rulings in English Law, definitions and precedents that America has followed since its founding.

The founders knew that the English common law evolved during the Middle Ages from rulings by the local church priests who used the 10 commandments and Jesus' law of love as their basis of law to make decisions. The priests were eventually replaced with the state's judges or king's judges - - - who still followed the common law and made the law via their rulings. Richard J. Maybury succinctly summarizes evolution of natural law that violates no religion into two simple TORT principles:

- *"Do all that you have agreed to do"*? This is the basis of Contract Law.

- *"Do not encroach on other persons or their property"*. This is basis of Criminal Law.

Richard Maybury's analysis mentions three types of wrongdoing. The first is bad manners where if no one notices, no harm is done. The second is sin, doing something that was forbidden by God in certain of his commandments. This concerns damage to yourself but not others. The third is *TORT, which is also a sin but is damage to others by the use of fraud, theft or force.* Some of the 10 commandments deal with sin against oneself and others deal with sins that are also TORTS. As an example, in England, where the founders' forbears came from, if you skipped Anglican services on Sunday, the English government picked you up and put you in jail. This practice was dropped in this country probably because it cost money for police to enforce crimes against oneself that harm no one else. The Juris Naturalists will only create laws that are TORTS, whereas others will try to control sins and criminalize crimes against oneself but are not torts.

Statists

The opposite of a Juris Naturalist is a Statist. *A statist believes that the government can perform services in which benefits are greater than the total costs.* Statism has become the de-facto policy of America. The government now provides economic services via social security, welfare, unemployment and social entitlements of pensions, Medicare and a long list of others. Since the middle 1980s, entitlement programs have accounted for more than half of all federal spending. For such entitlements Juris Naturalists ask, **"Where is the evidence of benefit?"** Their belief is that the hidden costs override the benefit and further that the government does nothing efficiently. This is one of the major issues surrounding a nationalized medical care system.

Political Power

Political power is the legal privilege of encroaching on the life, liberty and property of a person who has not harmed anyone. Only governments have this power and all politicians want to control this power. Governments can use force to enforce their rulings and this is what makes them different from men or other organizations. In private life and enterprise, there are two types of authority - the authority of position and the authority of knowledge. The only power one has over another is that which one allows and persuasion must be used to get that power. Government power uses force.

Freedom and Liberty

These terms often are used as if they have the same meaning but they have differences. *Liberty is the right granted by our creator.* Liberty was first defined in 490 BC when 10,000 Athenians, at the battle of Marathon, fought and defeated Darius and his 24,000 Persians with a loss of 219 Athenians and 6400 Persians. Darius came to defeat and enslave the Athenians. By using *"liberty"* as their battle cry, the Athenians rallied freemen because they knew that only the individual can give up his right to liberty and it was worth dying for. Athens then went on to define liberty and freedom in its art and thespian works. *Freedom*, on the other hand, has two meanings. *First, is the unalienable right from God to do something and second is permission from the state to do something.* Permission from the state means that men with political power can negate or compromise an individual's rights to liberty any time they can acquire political power to do so. It is up to the individual to fight for his rights for liberty.

Nature of Political Power

Political power is brute force. Governments can use brute force to enforce their rulings, which can be made into law or directives from agencies, which serve as de facto lawmakers with their rulings. They can send men with guns to enforce their policies. No other institution can do this. The government uses the power of taxing, conscription; laws against things that the politicians in power do not like such as drugs, alcohol, tobacco and gun ownership or that the politicians in power do like such as participation in social security, ethanol or health care plans. In contrast, religions use concepts to persuade and the concept - - "*do not encroach on other persons or their property.*" Both liberal and conservative politicians want political power and the right to enforce their ideas.

Categories of Encroachment

There are *two types of encroachment*. One is *economic containing such things as money, work, production, trade and investment*. The liberals tend to try to control these things. The conservatives tend to let you be free in the economic category. The other encroachment is *social which refers to everything else such as drugs, alcohol, entertainment, movies, gambling and sexual practices*. Here the liberals let you be free but the conservatives try to control you because many are considered "sins".

Privacy represents a major category of encroachment. Again, the political approach is different. Here the *liberals believe that you should have privacy in your social conduct but not your economic conduct*. They want to stamp out the economic inequality of wealth. They are statist in economic matters but juris naturalists in social matters. *Conservatives*, on the other hand, grant privacy in your financial conduct but not your social conduct. They want to stamp out sin. Sin is the offense against God represented in Christian doctrines. They are Juris Naturalists in economic matters and statists in social matters.

Lord Acton documented that political power corrupts everything it touches because political power is the privilege of encroaching on others who have harmed no one. Although Juris Naturalists are not in favor of poverty and drug addiction, they feel that if government gets involved the problem gets worse.

New World Order

The New World Order (NWO) is a Platonian system with a political ruler that can override all laws with his opinion. He acts as a king/emperor. The US operates with a Constitution and is a government of laws that all, including the President, must follow. The Platonian government is a centrist system where there are political leaders in power and uses a legislature to make laws. If he does not like those laws, he can override them. The New World Order follows the objectives of the illuminati, a secret organization. This group of people operates with a code of conduct that follows the illuminati creed. It organizes with circles within circles. Only the innermost circles know the true purpose of the organization. In our society, many organizations founded by the very rich operate this way. Some of the better known are Yale's Skull and Bones, the Council on Foreign Relations, the Club of Rome, the Trilateral Commission and the Bilderbergers. These organizations, objectives, organizations and identification of some of the principals are discussed in my book, **"Who's Next?"**[1]

Currently, the centralist NWO global organization appears to be global and has privately held institutions that they use or will use when they want to blossom the New World Order. It must have a central bank (IMF) that is advised by the Bank of International Settlements BIS. The IMF will control the privately held nation state central banks as the Federal Reserve System in the US or the Bank of England in the UK. The global money will be System Drawing Rights (SDR) issued by the IMF. These are nation state draws upon their privately held central bank. The nation state central bank will still create their fiat money but it will be valued against the SDR.

The SDR will be valued with a weighted average method of currently, US dollars (41.73%), European EUs (30.93%), Japanese Yen (8.33%), and ChineseRMB (10.92%) and Pound Sterling (8.09%). The corporations of the world will control the governments of the nation states. This is what the Trans Pacific Partnership (TPP) provides. The TPP is a trade agreement among twelve of the Pacifica Rim countries—notably not including China. The discussion and explanation of these relationships are out of scope of this study but are discussed in my book, **W ho's Next?**

For the NWO to be successful, the nation state will require beliefs in Communism/Socialism and Fascism at the state level. Communism is necessary since it requires centrist Socialism on a global rather than national scale and holds that there is no God just the state. Fascism is needed because the power centers will be concentrated into what I call in this book, the *"Group"*. Others call it the *"illuminati"* or *"conspirators"*. They operate through international organizations and national organizations previously mentioned. Members of the Group consist of representatives of few Wall Street Bankers, Oil magnates, and CEOs of transnational corporations. Most of them are senior members of the Council of Foreign Relations. Some of them are interior circle members. The CFR has 4,000 members. Only a few are in the interior circles. Servando Gonzalez provides a detailed analysis of the NWO in his recent book, **_Psychological Warfare and the New World Order.2_** In this detailed documentary book, he pulls no punches.

> *"This book is about a conspiracy . . . It is about a vast right-left wing conspiracy carried out by a group of criminal psychopaths without any ideology at all except maximum power and control. To carry out their plans, the conspirators usually resort to deception, coercion, extortion, usury, racketeering, Ponzi schemes, theft, torture, assassination and large – scale murder."*

Focus on the words *"right-left wing"* conspiracy. This is true but its meaning will not become clear until you see my circular scaling later in this book. He goes on and clarifies what he means.

> *"America is at war. But this not a conventional war waged with tanks, battleships and planes in conventional battlefields —at least not yet. It is a secret, insidious type of war whose battleground is the people's minds. Its main weapons are propaganda and mass brainwashing by disinformation, cunning, deception and lies in a large scale not used against the people of any nation since Nazi Germany. Though important, however, those elements are just part of a series of carefully planned and executed long and short-term psychological warfare operations. In synthesis, it is a psychological war —a PSY WAR. . . For almost a century, these small group of conspirators have been waging a quiet, non-declared war of attrition against the American people, and it seems that they are now ready for the final, decisive battle. Unfortunately, as the last two presidential elections showed, the brainwashed American people reacted by changing the puppets, leaving the puppet masters untouched and in control." - Servando Gonzalez*

These conspirators have set the illuminati goals to be achieved. The ultimate goal of these conspirators is the total destruction of the American Republic as we know it and the creation of a global communo-fascist feudal totalitarian society under their full control – a society they euphemistically call the New World Oder."3

The NWO control will reside in a relatively few firms and individuals but the intent is for these individuals to influence nations to become communist with the party leadership controlled by them on a global scale and the nations to become fascist states where the real power rests in the moneyed interests in the "Group" which are behind the nation states. The choice of Communism has two appeals to these men. It is Godless and it is international. These men are literally the "enemy within". Gore Vidal of Czechoslovakia, explains - *"Apparently, 'Conspiracy stuff', is now short hand for the unspeakable truth."*

ENGLISH MERCANTILE SYSTEM

In order to understand what is really happening here, we must step back in time to examine Mercantilism. The NWO "Group" is using a form of global Mercantilism that benefits themselves and not the countries involved. The English Mercantilism system was designed to help the mother country create a favorable balance of trade, favorable specie inflow, economic self-sufficiency and an export surplus. The Colonies were expected to supply products, which would otherwise have to be obtained from non-imperial sources, generate exports by the production and sale of products in high demand outside the empire, and provide a market for the mother country's exports. The mother country would provide the colonies with centralized governmental control of the economy, as well as naval and military protection.

The English laws that systematized these developments for North America were enacted as Navigation Acts from 1651 to about 1760. In 1696, laws were enacted where they confined the transport trade within the Empire to only British or colonial ships, required all exports from Europe to the colonies to be shipped via England (and vice versa), and specified a list of goods that could not be shipped to European ports - other than England. These included sugar, cotton, tobacco, indigo, wool, naval stores, rice, furs, and copper. By the mid-seventeenth century, the colonies were prosperous and were encouraged in their prosperity by credits from home. The plantation colonies especially fitted nicely into the mercantilist system because the economies of the South and Britain naturally complemented one another. Britain carried the burden of colonial defense and gave colonial goods and ships protection abroad.

In the early 1690s, England focused on a series of wars with France known as the French and Indian Wars in the Colonies. During this period, laws were evaded and systematic smuggling was occurring but confined mainly to tea and molasses. For the most part the mercantile system provided easy credit, assured commercial markets, and brought economic prosperity to colonies and mother countries alike. A summary of the main elements of the Mercantile system as practiced during colonial times follow:

- The Interests of the Nation Empire (England) are paramount

- The Government (England) and the economic sector work together to secure advantages in international trade – exporting more than you import – is crucial to national (England) success.

- A favorable balance of trade (England) – exporting more than you import - is crucial to national success.

- National wealth (England) is measured in Gold.

- Nations (England) must build navies to ensure sea routes as well as fight wars to ensure trade partners.

- Colonies must benefit the nation and not drain resources.

Mercantilism inevitably brought trade disputes with other countries, which in turn often degenerated into military struggles such as between England, France and Spain.

In 1776 economist Adam Smith (1723–1790), a Mercantile System critic, in his book, **Wealth of Nations**, defined a country's wealth in terms of labor and not money (gold). Smith advocated the free play of individual enterprise and free trade. Historians such as George Bancroft (1800–1891) condemned mercantilism as the source of foreign policy. He concluded that the Navigation Acts and mercantilism in general were the basic causes of the American Revolution (1775–1783). I believe that these were the stated reasons but that the American citizen was innately a believer in Liberty and

Freedom. They did not want the outside control of another nation such as England.

21ST CENTURY MERCANTILISM

Now let us focus on an updated Mercantilism. Recall that at the time of the American Revolution, British Mercantilism was in full bloom. The colonies supplied raw materials to the mother country, England; and then England manufactured goods and sent them to the colonies and Europe where they were consumed. The colonies were not allowed to manufacture the goods. The mother country became richer by acquiring and accumulating gold. This was the era of gold backed currency and not fiat currency.

Today, Transnational Firms including international banking and hedge funds who are members of the *"Group"* have replaced the mother country nation state. This is the cornerstone of the New World Order. It is a way to make money for the transnational firms by using the nation states as their *"colonies"*. The nation state is looked upon as a colony to the *"Group"*. The *"Group"* has no national allegiance because they consider themselves as globalists. Rather, the *"Group"* is chartered to maximize profits for their private corporate institutions by going from country to country if necessary. The idea is to Get raw materials from country A, manufacture in country B and sell products globally, which is maximizing their profits.

Under their new rules, the profit Interests of the Transnational *"Group"* are paramount. The Transnational *"Group"* and the economic sector of nation states work together to secure advantages in international trade for the Group. They are not constrained by national boundaries. Thus, exporting more than you import within a nation state – is not crucial to the *"Group's"* profit success. It is very crucial to the nation state.

The transnational firm manufactures in the low cost country, export to the larger market to maximize their profits with no consideration or obligation to any nation state or its citizens. Many examples exist but the recent multi-billion dollar bailout of European Central banks by the FED is blatant. Only the international bankers benefitted - - - they stayed in business and the US taxpayers took on their bad debts due to bad management of the banks. The transnational banks have a win-win business. If they make profits, they win and keep them. If they have losses, the citizens bail them out and they win again. This is the reason they do not like competition and smaller banks. Since 2007 when the new depression began, they have closed over 2,000 banks and acquired their assets. During the great Depression, the number was 5,000.

Recall that during the 18th century Mercantile system, a favorable balance of trade (England) – exporting more than you import - was crucial to national solvency and success. The modern **"Group"** does not care about that. The transnational firms only care about using the Nation states to maximize their profits stemming from their transnational operations. For example, even though the firm's mother country is the US, they manufacture in China and ship to the US, which maximizes China'sBalance of Payments (BOP), reduces the US Balance of Payments, reduces employment in the US, increases employment in China but maximizes the *"Group's"* profits.

"Group" wealth is measured in increases in Owner's Equity in the *"Group"* rather than accumulation of Gold in the state as in the original mercantilism. The Transnational firms become larger.

Nations such as England and the US must build navies to ensure sea routes. However, the "Group" has figured out how to get Nations such as US to have the navies and armies, fight wars that ensure that their trade routes are secure and incur the expenses of war so that Group's profits are maximized. The nation state incurs the costs and the Group keeps the profits. The US spent over $2 trillion in Iraq/Afghanistancosting10, 000 men killed, 25,000 wounded or crippled and the "Group", in this instance, Shell, Exxon Mobil, British Petroleum, Anadarko and Dome (UAE) got 30% of all oils from Iraq in the post war agreement. Note that only one firm is U.S. based. The U.S. nation state was not even paid back their expenses. The oil went to private mostly European companies.

The message is clear - Nations must benefit the *"Group"* and not drain resources of the *"Group"*. The big companies get bigger. Politicians stay in office. The assets of the power structure increase and the private citizen pays more taxes.

The reader should note that the above charter, when extended globally, requires a combination of Communism and Fascism. The *"Group"* accomplished its ends by encouraging with money centrist socialism in the Nation, fascism in the country and extension of socialism to other nations. This then becomes National Socialism globally. This is precisely what Hitler wanted. A centrist government is easier to control and get to fight the necessary wars for profit that the *"Group"* wants and needs. The world rejected this in W WII but the modern world seems to be accepting this charter.

The above is the charter for the New World Order that is promoted by the Council of Foreign Relations in speeches before the CFR and articles in their Foreign Affairs magazine. Most of the time, it is not stated in these clear terms. Nonetheless, this is the agenda.

The NWO intent is to create a communo-fascist state where the *"Group"* of international firms benefit and manage the world of Nations - - - the modern colonies - - - and, it is believed, that this *"Group"* is controlled by less than a 1,000 old families of the world that belong to the Committee of 300. See **Conspirators Hierarchy: The Story of the Committee of 30 0**by John Coleman for a detailed clarification.4See my book, *Who's Next?*,for an organization chart of how the Group works.

POLITICAL SPECTRUM

The above provides a necessary background for what follows. Richard Maybury, Carroll Quigley5and many others hold that America has in fact a one party system. Both the Republicans and the Democrats are controlled by special interests. Today these interests are clearly the industrial complexes of banking/insurance, judicial/prison, labor unions, pharmaceutical /medical as well as the military industrial complex. The particular influential industry varies with time and the event being considered in Congress.

Politicians from both parties vie to get into office so that they have the power of government to enforce their views. The result is that, regardless of the party in power, this increases the scope and size of government. Historically, we know that when government increases in size, scope and power, individual liberties are lost. At each election, no matter who gets into power, government will grow and the citizen's liberties will become fewer.

ConsiderRonald Reagan as an example of onewho tried to reduce government but all he could do was slow its growth. **Exhibit 1, ANOTHER POLITICAL SPECTRUM,** below provides some insight as to where the terms defined above fit and what the current political spectrum looks like in America. If one believes that corporate special interests now control both parties, then America has become a de-facto controlled society and the stage has been set for the New World Order. The term usually reserved for this type of control is fascism. It does not bother the corporate fascist interests (*"Group"*) that the current elected President is Democratic, Republican, Socialist or Communist in their beliefs. It only is important that they can affect and control his policies and make money from those policies. The politicians want to be elected so that they can enforce their ideas using Government force. I agree with Maybury when he calls fascist politicians *"people in a hurry"* to get others to accept their beliefs.

The Fascists, who generally made their wealth and position using the capitalist system, are now more interested in maintaining their *"king of the mountain"* status via affecting control of government with the politicians that they help put into office. Recently, another goal, institute a New World Order, has been introduced and promoted via the Tri Lateral Commission, Council of Foreign Relations along with strategically placed billionaire *"assets"* who spend generously to affect socialistic liberal politics. As long as the corporate transnational fascists remain in control, they promote and sell the current government as a good form of government.

Let us now look at Exhibit 1, Another Political Spectrum. This measurement puts all the definitions that we have discussed on a single scale. When one considers this scale, one can realize the complexity of the American political belief system. To me that is healthy. It takes multiple opinions in a great society to make the nation strong. Now let us examine the scale more closely.

EXHIBIT 1, ANOTHER POLITICAL SPECTRUM

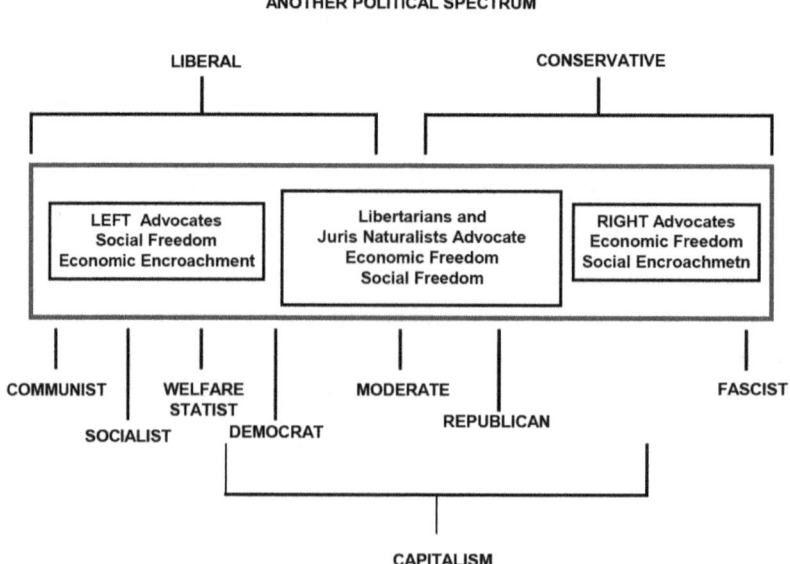

The Middle Ground

The political spectrum of beliefs is broken into three parts: the left, the right and the moderates in the middle. The right advocates economic freedom and social encroachment. The left advocates social freedom and economic encroachment. The Centrists in the Moderate middle advocate both economic and social encroachment. At either extreme, one has communist or fascist who advocate limited freedom and State centralist directed control from a top down government. The communists differ from the socialists in that they want to extend their control to all nations not just one. We currently have a fascist controlled government that has large transnational corporations affecting the laws (Obamacare, Dodd Frank, TPP, NAFTA) in a way to maximize their profits at the expense of the citizens.

Republicans and Democrats

A central concept that one must remember about politicians is that they want the office in order to have the power to enforce their ideas with force if necessary. As a result, no matter who wins, both parties increase the power of government because that is the instrument that they use to make certain that their ideas are enforced on the people. I agree with Maybury in his belief that the political parties are marketing organizations. They package and promote candidates that they believe can be elected. They need to market themselves and appeal to the electorate. The parties from election to election choose to set their platforms to appeal more to the left or right. Generally, the Democrats lean to the Left and the Republicans lean to the right. Maybury points out that once elected they oftentimes do odd things. For instance, a Liberal Lyndon Johnson sends troops to war in Vietnam and a Conservative Bush enacts liberal wage-price controls. Why? The test that works generally is to - - - " *follow the money*"! The fascist elements that make money off the event promoted by the administration want it but will never admit to influencing the event. However, they do *"favors"* for the administration.

Republican Democracy

A democracy requires direct election of the legislature. Our founders feared this sort of government because it led to tyranny. They chose a Republic that had three partitions in government. Specifically, a House directly elected, a Senate with <u>elected members from State legislatures</u>, an Executive and an independent Judiciary appointed for life by the President but vetted by the Senate. The XVII Amendment provided for the direct election of the Senate during the Wilson administration, in 1913. This was the same year that the FED and the IRS was created. They followed the path probably planned for at the 1910 Jekyll Island meeting. See my book, ***Who's Next?*** for details. Technically then, we ceased being a Republic in 1913 when the 17th Amendment was passed.

CHAPTER 3

IS AMERICA SOCIALIST, FASCIST, A DEMOCRATIC REPUBLIC or A NEW WORLD ORDER STATE?

THE "ISMS"

In this section, we review what I call the "isms". They are the convenient categories of political associations that we group people and their beliefs and practices.

Capitalism

Immigrants from Europe founded America. They fled that continent for one that provided religious and economic freedom. The Puritans first tasted economic freedom. Most Americans, who celebrate Thanksgiving, do not know that the Puritan Thanksgiving was actually in their second year on the new continent and going into their third winter. The first year was a catastrophe. You see, the first year was organized as a collectivist colony – each family joined other families and collectively fished, made goods and farmed as a ***"team"***. Because of the nature of man, some were slackers and the good producers soon found out that their extra work and productivity led to no more from the common store.

The Puritans landed in the fall and had enough to get through the first winter. They planted their first crops as a collectivist team and their collectivist work did not provide enough to last the second winter. Because of this, one-half of the Puritans starved to death that second winter. This was after their first socialist harvest. Governor Braddock, their leader, said, *"This is not working. Let us divide the common land into parcels and let each family have a parcel."*

The rest is history; they produced more than they could eat using a free enterprise capitalist system; invited the Indians, who had shown them how to plant maize, to share their harvest; gave thanksgiving to God and they never starved again. In fact, by the third year, they were shipping goods and foods back to Europe for sale. This enticed other Europeans to come to this new *"Land of Opportunity"*. Thus, was established the Protestant work ethic, free enterprise and capitalism that that made this nation.

The Capitalism established by our founders in America is a system based on four simple principles:

- Freedom of choice
- Private property rights
- Profit motive of owners - self interest
- Owner control of production

Capitalism works and socialism and Communism do not for two reasons, one is because no production set of decisions can optimally be made by committee in one central place without the use of private property and pricing. The second is that capitalism harnesses self-interest in the human psyche. A privately owned business is the antithesis to a government controlled socialist or communist owned business. In the latter form, *"government" replaces "owner"*. In an individually owned business –

- The owner is responsible for management, all operational decisions, and sets business policies.

- The owner supplies or borrows the capital; is responsible for all debts; receives all profits earned.

- No special legal formalities are required to form a business other than purchase of a business permit, or pay local license fees.

- The life of the business is tied to the life of the owner. It continues until the owner sells it, retires or dies.

This was the type of business that made this nation. Virtually, all of the founders were either farmers, business owners or doctors who owned their own businesses. What happened when the capitalist economic system was used? This nation was successful and eventually grew into a free enterprise manufacturing giant such that after W WII, we did most of the world's manufacturing.

Welfare Statism

This is a form of socialism that is common in the United States today. It started in the 30s and 40s and is associated with J. Maynard Keynes, a communist atheist economist, who promoted government involvement in the private sector to *"stimulate the economy"*. Such things as Social Security, Medicare, and Aid to Families with Dependent Children fall into this category. Prior to the 1930s, few people believed in these concepts; rather, they believed in Christian charity to help others in need.

During the Depression, unemployment grew to 37.5% by 1939. During the Depression, people got frightened and accepted the government social security as a *"safety net"*. Many social programs followed that were defined by the political followers of Keynes. These men believed in centrist welfare socialist government. The irony is that millions of GIs have been sent around the world to fight Communism when socialism, a necessary predecessor to Communism, was taking over the US.

Socialism and Communism

Today, many believe that socialism is just another form of advanced liberalism. Generally, a socialist wants government power over our individual wealth so that, in his mind, the inequality of wealth can be greatly reduced and poverty can be eliminated. They also want to destroy private property and capitalism. Their beliefs have recently been epitomized in Obama's statement that we need to, **"Spread the wealth around"**. Socialism is the antithesis of what drives entrepreneurs and what made this nation. Profits drive the capitalist system and self-interest makes it succeed.

LENIN'S TEN POINT PROGRAM FOR COMMUNISM

At this point, it is instructive to review the Leninist 10 point program for collectivism or Communism. They are stated here as well as observations made where the US and China are in relation to the ten points. Why China? It is a Communist nation and the US is a Capitalist nation. The contrast show how close we are to Communism. Here is Lenin's 10-point program that must be completed prior to Communism being instituted:

Are You Liberal? Libertarian? Conservative? or Confused?

1. Abolition of property in land and application of all rents of land to public purposes

In this US, this has not taken place yet.

In China, the Government owns all land and the state makes all Bureaucrats personally responsible for the proper stewardship of the land's usage. Today, farmers are allowed to pass the land from generation to generation but are the state's property. If the Bureaucrat fails, they are usually imprisoned or executed.

2. A heavy progressive or graduated income tax

In the US, we have a progressive Federal Income Tax since 1913. It is in direct conflict with the Constitution that says that there is to be no personal tax. It was probably part of the plan of the 1910 Jekyll Island meeting.

In China, t*here is no sales tax; it appears that Corporations pay most taxes as an income tax.* A number of the larger corporations are state owned.

3. Abolition of all right of inheritance

In the US, the inheritance tax of 2011 has been renewed.

In China, there is no Inheritance tax. Farming land rights are assigned to the family for its use. After death, the rights are transferred to the family members. This is de-facto capitalism in practice. However, it reserves the right for the state to take their property back.

4. Confiscation of the property of all emigrants and rebels.

In the US, RICO law exists for rebels. However, they must be convicted in a fair trial. Emigrants from US citizenship are now paying stiff penalties for this inalienable right.

In China, confiscation must occur only after the defendants are proven guilty of a felony.

5. Centralization of credit in the hands of the State, by means of a national bank with State capital and an exclusive monopoly.

In the US, the FED (a private banking cartel) was given control of all financial institutions by the 2010 Dodd/ Frank Finance law. The government supports the bank losses in the case of failure. Large banks will not be allowed to fail. This is written into the law if they qualify as being **"Too big to fail."**

In China, the State recommends a credit policy to publicly owned banks operating in China. If the bank does not comply and fails, the Government will not support their losses. This is capitalism. The US policy is socialism.

6. Centralization of the means of communication and transport in the hands of the State.

In the US, our public press is free but today is controlled by a group of five owners. Internet is free but can be shut down anytime due to the recent Obama executive order for the "switch". In US, transportation, railroads, buses and airlines are privately owned.

In China, communications are controlled about the same as in the U.S. Google recently got back its license. In China, transportation and railroads are owned and operated by the Government. Most airlines, buses, and taxis are privately owned.

7. Extension of factories and instruments of production owned by the State; the bringing into cultivation of waste - lands, and the improvement of the soil generally in accordance with a common plan.

In the US, most manufacturing for consumer goods is done in China, a Communist country. In addition, the US government now controls GM-manufacturing, AIG-insurance, and banking and has shut down drilling in the Gulf and portions of the north slope of Alaska. The state via the President is imposing its rules on the free market.

In China, most farming is done on family "owned" land. All land is government owned but given to a family to farm. Farming assistance is offered to the farmers as well as low interest loans for farm equipment, but no quotas are assigned. Much manufacturing is owned and operated by "on-duty" military personnel. They just go to work in civilian clothes. The military colleges have taught their officers to become good leaders and managers. This talent has been applied to China's rapid growth in manufacturing. No business permits or licenses are required for businesses in China. Many of these Chinese officers have become millionaires. Certain sectors are emphasized by supplying capital and allowing entities to grow as in a capitalist society.

8. Equal liability (financially and legally responsible for something) of all to labor. InEstablishment of industrial armies, especially for agriculture.

In the US, unions are not that strong yet but have made major inroads with government during the Obama administration.

China: Almost all unions have been installed in foreign owned companies. Wal-Mart was unionized about a year ago.

9. Combination of agriculture with manufacturing industries; gradual abolition of the distinction between town and country, by a more equitable distribution of the population over the country.

In the US, there have been movements from large cities to smaller towns.

In China, there are 800 million people on farms, and 400 million people in cities making more money. A large portion of the 800 million people wants to move to the cities. The government is spending money to raise the income and standard of living in the countryside with the goal of reducing the migration.

10. Free education for all children in public schools. Abolition of children's factory labor in its present form. Combination of education with industrial production.

In the US, free public schools exist. However, the quality is questionable. Children factory labor has been stopped.

In China, there are both public and private schools that teach the arts, technology, and agriculture. It is not unusual for a gifted Chinese student to study classical piano at a private high school for music. A Chinese student can get free college training if they pass an extensive test. Otherwise, they pay for a private college education. English is taught as a second language in all schools. A point to ponder is that there is more Chinese studying English today than there are people in the United States. Many Chinese like to demonstrate their knowledge of English by greeting Americans in English.

If one studies the above, one recognizes that the US has moved toward collectivism, which has proved to be unsuccessful and cataclysmic for society while China is moving toward free enterprise at the commercial and industrial levels since they have found

Communism not as economical or productive for their people. The Chinese communist party maintains political level national party control with a very small party membership. Thus, the politicians at the top continue to maintain power but recognize that free enterprise at middle class and lower daily levels satisfies their people and keeps them happy.

According to the Engels and Marx's Communist Manifesto in 1848, the above steps were prior conditions for a transition from capitalism to Communism. The conflict between Capitalism and Socialism would lead to Communism. A chief element of Marxist theory was the economic interpretation of history. Marx derived from Hegel what philosophers call the *"historical dialectic"*. This theory maintains that all historical events are a struggle between opposing forces, which ultimately merge to forge a situation that was different from either. This represents the classical thesis (capitalism) and antithesis (socialism) and then the synthesis (Communism) of ideas. Marx believed that the economic organization of any society was the critical aspect of society since all other aspects, such as political, social, intellectual or religious reflected the organization and powers of the economic level.

Karl Marx believed that society moved through several stages before it got to communism. These are - 1. Primitive slave state; 2. Feudalism; 3. Mercantilism; 4. Capitalism; 5. Socialism; 6. Communism. Communism was the utopian end-stage of socialism in which government has vanished and we live as happy individuals cooperating with one another. In essence, we live happily together under the rule, **"from each according to his ability, to each according to his need"**. This concept has only seemed to work in a few monasteries, and gatherings of idealists. It did not work for the Puritans. Communism is an ideal in which there is no government. Politicians in the USSR are no different from other politicians. They seek political power. Communism was their means and excuse to come to power. The USSR was a tyranny.

Marxist theory says socialism is a transitional stage between capitalism and Communism. The purpose of socialism is to prepare the way for Communism. This justifies taking whatever brutal means are required to make socialism work. The Soviet Union was used as a test bed and it collapsed. Europe is both socialist and communist. Under socialism, they have a lesser standard of living than the US.

FASCISM AND NAOMI WOLF'S 10 REQUIRED STEPS

It is apparent to critical observers that America is becoming a Fascist state in several ways. How did this happen? Naomi Wolf wrote an explanatory article in The UK Guardian, 24 April 2007 called "Fascist America, in 10 easy steps"6, that provides the 10 steps that must take place to create a Fascist state. This describes what has been happening in the US. Briefly, we will list and comment on Naomi Wolf's 10 required steps to enable Fascism.

1. Invoke a Terrifying Internal and External Enemy

After 9/11/01, the enemy was the Al Qaida terrorists. However, this time the war was never ending and encompassed the earth. No other war that America has entered has been like this. After other wars, freedom returned. It is important to note that Hitler used the communists and then the Jews as the threat to Germany. *Completed*

2. Create a Gulag

Once you have everyone scared, create a prison system outside the rule of law. This prison system allows the rulers to insert citizens for violating their arbitrary rules. Two examples exist, Guantanamo, where "torture" exists. However, these are wartime combatants not civilian criminals. On the other hand we have unused to date *"concentration camps"* exposed by many on the internet. These were built by Halliburton to house millions, exposed, and photographed by Jesse Ventura and others. On April 24, 1934, the NAZIs established the **"People's Court"** which bypassed the judicial system and their constitution. We don't have that yet; however, we now have executive orders that have removed the habeas corpus and unlawful search rights. The next step is simply the *"People's Court"*. <u>Completed</u>

3. Develop a Thug Caste

When the political leaders wanted a fascist shift, they established *"Blackshirts"* in Italy and *"Brownshirts"* in Germany. These organizations were used to intimidate the population under the guise of looking for communists and terrorists. It appears that the US created such a private army in IRAQ and Afghanistan with the Xe organization that now works for Monsanto. These contractors were immune from prosecution and outside of U.S. and Iraqi law. They worked for the State Department. One could make a case that similar organizations exist in the relatively recent creation of the ATF and the TSA. All report to the President and not the DOD. <u>*Completed*</u>

4. Set up An Internal Surveillance System

The Patriot Act allows unlimited surveillance of emails and wiretaps under the cover of national security. Is this in fact a way to detect dissenters and inhibit their activism? Has NSA set up such surveillance? They have the technology but no one knows.

5. Harass Citizen's Groups

Related to step 4, you now infiltrate and harass citizen groups. The ACLU reports that thousands of anti-war, environmental and dissenting groups have been infiltrated. A Counterintelligence Field

Activity Agency of DOD has been gathering activities on domestic organizations engaged in peaceful political activities. It theory, it tracks "potential terrorist threats". The IRS harassed TEA party groups. <u>Completed</u>

6. Engage In Arbitrary Detention and Release

This scares people. You have lists of people who are harassed by the Government. The TSA currently has such suspected "terrorist" lists and deny people access to flying or detains and harasses them when trying. Have you been on a Peace March? You will be on the list. <u>Completed</u>

7. Target Key Individuals

Threaten professionals such as civil servants, academics and artists with loss of their job if they do not abide with the government's position. Mussolini went after the rectors of state universities if they did not conform to the fascist line. Bush supporters in state legislatures put pressure on the academics of state universities who had been critical of the administration. It now appears as if Obama / Hillary supporters have targeted news media organizations. <u>Unknown</u>

8. Control the Press

All would be dictators target newspapers and journalists. Currently, they are wondering how to control the internet. They threaten and harass Journalists. Homeland security brought a criminal complaint against reporter Greg Palast, claiming that he threatened *"critical infrastructure"* when he filmed victims of Hurricane Katrina in Louisiana. Greg Palast had written a best seller, *The Best Democracy Money Can Buy*,critical of the Bush administration. Finally, this election cycle clearly shows the press as anti-Trump. <u>Completed</u>

9. Dissent Equals Treason

Cast dissent as "treason" and criticism as "espionage". All closing societies use this technique. In Stalin's Soviet Union, dissidents were *"enemies of the people"* and National Socialists called those who supported the Weimer Democracy, *"November Traitors"*. In September 2006, Congress passed the Military Commissions Act of 2006, in which the President has the power to call any US Citizen an *"enemy combatant"*. He also has the power to define, *"enemy combatant"*. He has the power to seize you, incarcerate you and keep you isolated. The Center for Constitutional Rights state the Bush administration was actively looking for ways to get around the right to trial for American Citizens. Americans donot seem to get the impact of this yet. In every closing society, at a certain point, there will be some high profile arrests – usually of opposition leaders, clergy and journalists. Julian Assange, of Wiki Leaks, could be one. After the arrests, the press remains but real dissent disappears. History shows, that this is where we are today. **Completed**

10. Suspend the Rule of Law

The John Warner Defense Act of 2007 gave the president new powers over the National Guard. Specifically, in a state of emergency that he personally can declare, he can send the National Guard of Michigan to enforce a state of emergency in Oregon - - - over the objections of the people and Governors in both states. This is precisely how China suppressed dissidents at Tiananmen Square. They brought in troops from western China that did not speak the local dialect. The New York Times notes that *"in the middle of the night"* laws were enacted that now allow military troops to be used as a domestic peace force. This is a clear violation of the Posse Comitatus Act enacted after the Civil War to remove the military from the South. The founders were terrified of military occupation. This is the type of law that removes the military from civilian law enforcement. The founders suffered under occupation before the revolution. **Completed**

Based on this analysis of 9 points, it appears that a process of layered erosion of our freedoms has introduced Fascism. The men in control of this country are *"boiling the frog slowly"*. When this finally becomes understood, recall James Madison, the author of the Constitution, who said, " *The accumulation of all powers, in the same hands . . . is the definition of tyranny"*.We still have the choice whether we want to continue down this path or challenge it and change it. However, if we do not change the path, our republic will end and the US will end up as a fascist or communist dictatorship, which is what the New World Order wants,and we will find that our individual freedoms will be gone.

AN EXPANDED POLITICAL SPECTRUM

Our Founders were Juris Naturalists. Libertarians hold the same beliefs that are in the center of our scale. The Juris Naturalists combine Left and Right but are different from moderates. The Jurist Naturalists combine the Left's desire for Social Liberty and the Right's desire for Economic Liberty but they want little or no state encroachment. Moderates accept Economic and Social encroachment. In contrast, Statists want a Centrist government with virtually complete encroachment. Exhibit 2, DETAILED POLITICAL SPECTRUM, shows the relationships among these concepts.

EXHIBIT 2, AN EXPANDED POLITICAL SPECTRUM

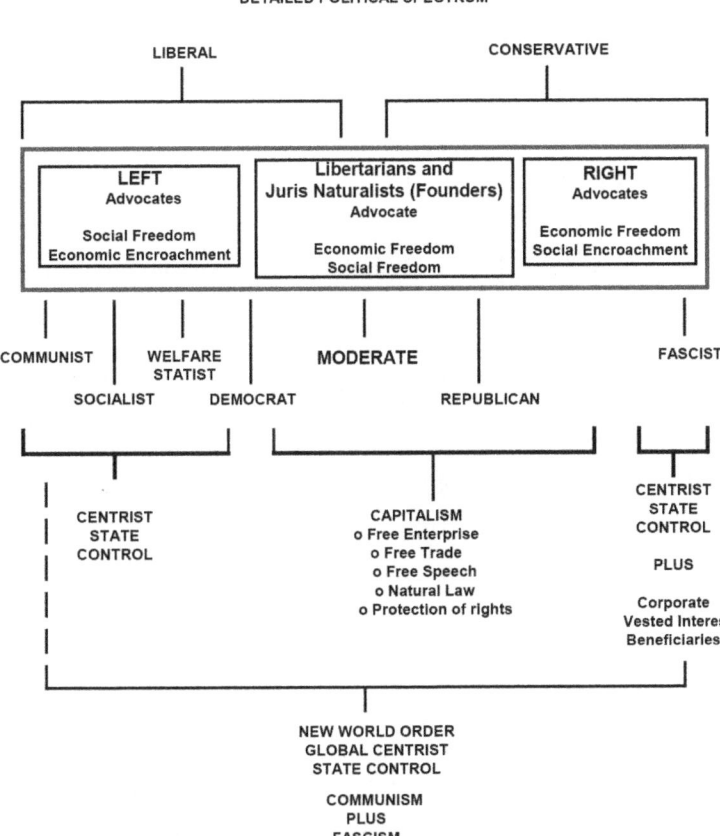

Sam Adams defines Juris Naturalists rights in this manner –

> *"The Natural Rights of the colonists are these: first a right to life; second, to liberty; third to property; together with the right to support and defend them in the best manner they can."*

Note that Sam Adams says life, liberty, property and to defend them in the best manner they can which includes the right to bear arms to protect these rights. Today, Supreme Court rulings have removed the protection of the right to property (Kelo v City of New London, Feb 2, 2005) and currently many in Congress are attempting to remove the right to bear arms and the right to not have warrantless searches. Over the last 50 years, our liberties from birth to death have gradually been removed or constrained by rulings from the Supreme Court as well as the Congress.

NEW WORLD ORDER

We can now discuss the components required for what the CFR, President Bush, Sr, and others refer to as the *"New World Order"*. What kind of political organization will exist in the sovereign nations belonging to this new world order of things? Exhibit 2 shows that it requires both Communism and fascism. How is that possible? Let us see how this comes together.

Intellectual Leadership

It is interesting to observe that Fascism has no intellectual leadership. Adam Smith is the Conservative and Libertarian intellectual and Karl Marx is the Socialists and Communist intellectual. It turns out that Fascists are anti-intellectual; they honor only power; truth is relative and a matter of opinion; therefore, right and wrong are also because <u>only action counts</u>. The fascist wants and respects power; might makes right. Thus, the only thing that counts is who wins. Mussolini was the first fascist. Hitler admired Mussolini so much that he made Germany a fascist state. He had a state that was both socialist and fascist. He allowed God but still had the Luftwaffe attack many churches in Poland.

In Fascism, the central government controls everything in the state similar to a socialist state but special interest large corporations that, for this paper, we will call the "Group" back the state. Today, most large firms are transnational. America is gradually becoming and in many ways has become a fascist driven state, which means that private corporations work in open and loose collusion with the state and the legislature. Because of this, the government makes laws benefitting certain sectors of private enterprise in a manner that enable them to make more money. In return, the private companies support the administration and Congress.

Think in terms of the banking bailout $700 billion TARP program and the pharmaceutical / insurance industrial complex in the $1 trillion Obama Care legislation. Also, consider that the military industrial complex that has been supporting and has been supported by the government since the 40s. Neither party's planned austerity program touches the Defense budget. Fascists consider the country and the government as *"one"* that they call the *"state"*. The Fascist political leader cares nothing about right or wrong, good or evil; rather, they care in only what is necessary to retain power. Mussolini understood this as evidenced by his statement, **"We have buried the putrid corpse of liberty"**.

In Italy, he made all the decisions and he decided what was necessary. Under fascism, if lying appears necessary, the fascist will lie; If truth appears necessary, the fascist will tell the truth; if freedom appears necessary, freedom is given; If slavery appears necessary, then slavery it is. Who is to say it is wrong? The head of state who was the emperor under Roman law makes the critical decisions. This is a Plato philosophy of government and not the one that is embedded in our constitution. Truth and justice are a matter of opinion. It is almost redundant to say those in power will do anything to stay there. The rule of Natural law reverts to Roman law when the emperor is substituted for God in Natural Law. It is the right of the Emperor to override Natural Law with nothing but his opinion that is always biased in order to keep himself in power.

Maybury noted that the most interesting and undermining characteristic of Fascism is that it can appear as any other philosophy.

Fascists are masters of disguise. He noted that the sad truth is that Hitler lost and died but the basic system of fascism and National Socialism that he fought for has swept the world. Why? Those desiring a New World Order must have these two systems.

For those readers that disagree, let us digress for a moment and listen to political debate in the US. The basic premise is that power holders should do what is necessary not what is right or wrong. They only disagree on the details. No one refers to the principles that made this nation other than Ron Paul. The determinant of right and wrong is what the majority says - - -nothing more. In Germany, the people fell into the trap of what the majority wanted not questioning whether it was right or wrong. As a result, they ended up with death camps, which evolved from the German 1939 Tiergarten IV program whose medical review boards led to 282,000 German civilian deaths over the next five years.

These deaths were not in Concentration camps. Why were these German citizens killed? The answer is that their fascist leaders did what was necessary when they saw that these Germans were "*useless eaters*" and could not contribute to the war effort. These medical review boards showed up again in the Obama Care bill and Sarah Palin labeled them correctly as "*death panels*". The Nuremberg trials indicted, convicted and put to death 16 of the 25 physicians who served on those German medical review board "*death panels*". The doctors' defense was that they just obeyed the German law and were in fact correct but the Prosecution said that they violated a higher law - Natural Law. Since there was a Russian on the panel, I believe that they discussed this and finally settled on the charger that they called "*crimes against humanity.*" This is where the phrase first entered our culture.

Fascists like Roman law because although Rome had a constitution and Roman law and refers to God as Jupiter, under Roman Natural Law the emperor actually overruled natural law (Jupiter). At that point, Roman law becomes the arbitrary law of a man and not written constitutional law. The founders tried to eliminate this possibility by defining principles for the Constitution in the Declaration of Independence; designing and writing a constitution to limit the powers allowed by the government including the Executive; and placing the nation and the Constitution under Common and Natural Law. This was unique in that America is the only government established based on a set of principles in the history of man. This Constitution established constraints on government that were based on the principles set forth in the Declaration of Independence. Politicians and jurists in power over the years have gradually expanded the government to a point where one can justify saying that we now, at times, have evolved to a form of Roman law in our government.

Test for Socialism and Fascism

Remember Representative Pelosi's (CA) infamous statement, *"We will find out what the law (Obama Care) says after it is passed."* Does this type of statement represent Socialism or Fascism – both Centrist? A test to determine the answer is to ask who benefits by the rule - - - *"Follow the money"*. The pharmaceutical and insurance companies pick up 10 to 20 million new illegal aliens at $1,000 / year or $10 to $20 billion for each industry. The $1,000 is paid for by the US government and the illegal aliens obviously benefit; also, the Congressional sector that promotes this law believes that they will benefit by additional *"bought"* votes and the industry benefits with more sales and profits. This passes the test for Fascism - - - favored private interest corporations get the profits and the government / people incur the costs. If all the tax-paying citizens benefited, then the case is made that it was socialism. The result is that the taxpayers pick up the costs of the illegal aliens and get no benefit for doing so.

New World Order Currency and Banking

When one considers the NWO, one must think international. Thus, the ideal for the promoters of the NWO is a global central bank such as the International Monetary Fund (IMF). This bank serves the same functions as the FED and the Bank of England does within their sovereign nations. Thus, it would create a currency similar to the dollar. It already exists and is called the SDR. Bankers have proposed that the SDR serve as an international currency between sovereign nations. The nations of the world would measure their currency in relation to the international SDR. Of course, another Bretton Woods of international states would be required so that they could all agree to fixed ratio of their currencies to the SDR. Alternatively, the sovereign nations' currencies could float against the SDR. In this manner, there would exist an international currency agreed to by all. The problem is that the individual states would have to give up some of their sovereignty in that they would lose significant control of their own currency. This is precisely what the NWO promoters want.

International Army

All governments use force to enforce their laws and rulings. A global government needs an army. Ideally, the NWO would have its own army to enforce its laws. An interim step would be to use international treaty organizations to gather the various sovereign nation forces in order to carry out their desires. Note that Korea was a UN peacekeeping action and not a war declared by Congress. The Iraq action was UN. The Afghanistan and Libya operation was NATO. Congress has not declared war per the constitution. Nonetheless, G.I.s were killed and maimed for the international cover operations that arguably had nothing to do with U.S. security. These actions set the precedents of commitment of troops to actions of international operations without Congressional direct approval and thereby bypassing the Constitution and our sovereign rights as a nation.

NWO Political Structure

A better depiction of the New World Order is provided in Exhibit 3, DETAILED POLITICAL SPECTRUM SHOWING THE NEW WORLD ORDER. The major differences between Exhibit 2 and 3 is that the scale has been folded into a circle. In this manner, one can see where the two extremes meet and see the conditions for meeting. The conditions are that the nation must become atheist and then the state/emperor/president can be substituted into Natural Law. This in turns degrades Natural Law into Roman law. In order to do that the state does not have to become completely atheist, rather the state will be run as if it were atheist. There will be no liberty since state rights always takes precedence over individual rights. Think in terms of Rome in the years 200 – 300 AD. The minority Christians were there and abided by Natural Law with Jupiter as God even though they believed Jesus was God. They were not in control until Constantine came to the throne. At the point when Constantine made Natural Law accept Jesus as God over Jupiter in the national religion, the Christians became a majority. The result will be that the nation must become socialist with the government controlling the individual and fascist where the "Group" will control the state. Thus, the "Group" will de-facto control the individual resulting of individual freedoms and liberty dying.

Supra National Trade Policies

The NWO countries will be organized into regional economic blocks that have already been identified as Americas, Europe, Africa and Asia. These blocks will adhere to the NWO directives of the supranational trade agreements. These already exist for the U.S. These agreements were imposed on Americans by the Administration and not voted upon by the citizens. Most were not even discussed in the open press. These are the NAFTA, North American Union, UN agreements such as the small arms treaty, Free Trade, TPP and outsourcing; none of which require votes by the citizens; all of which benefit the *"Group"* more than citizens. The net result is that jobs are lost, businesses are closed, unemployment is up but the transnational *"Groups'"* profits are up. The NWO only benefits the transnational corporations that are in the *"Group"*. It is not by accident that *"Group"* companies are well represented at the international conferences such as the Bilderbergers.

With this background, we cannot develop a scale that includes the New World Order and puts everything together. It is shown in Exhibit 3, Detailed Political Spectrum showing the New World Order.

ARE YOU LIBERAL? LIBERTARIAN? CONSERVATIVE? OR CONFUSED?

EXHIBIT 3, EXPANDED SPECTRUM WITH NEW WORLD ORDER

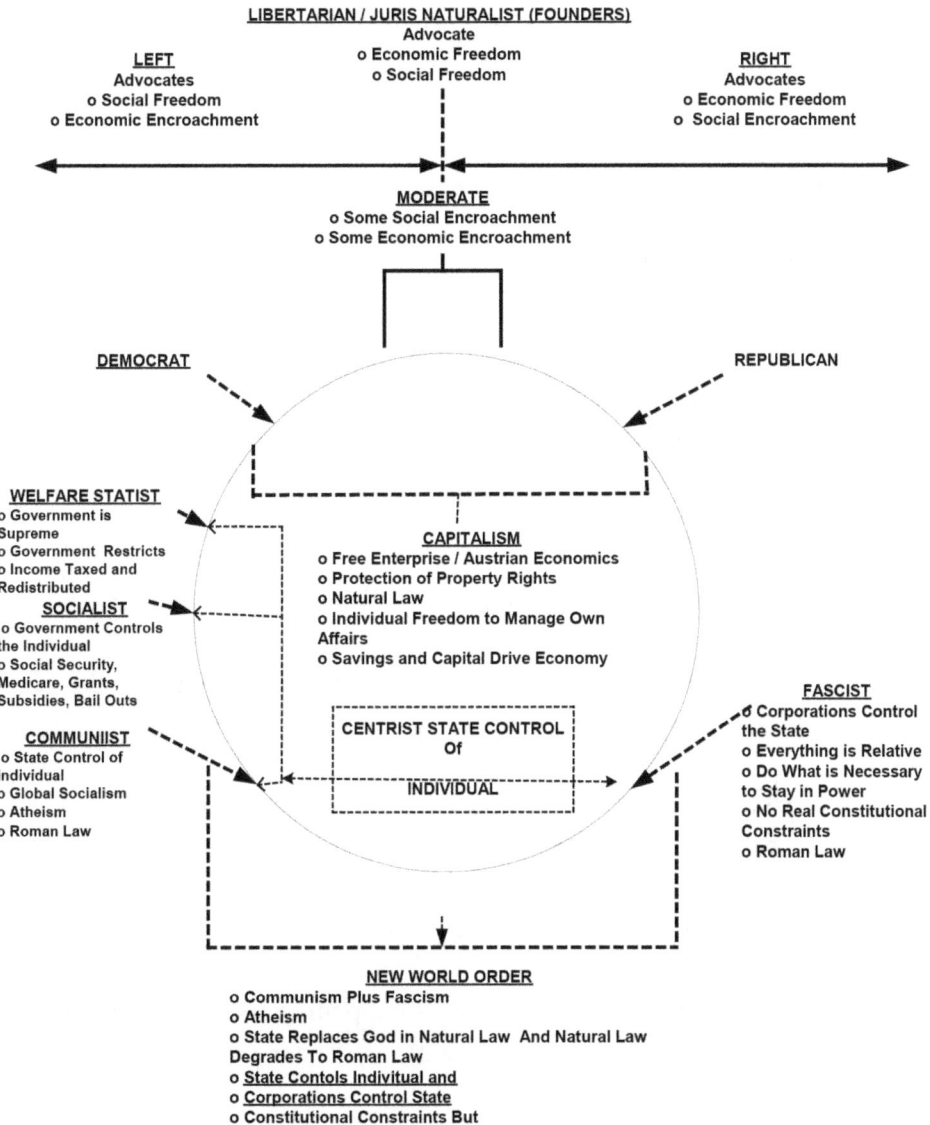

ECONOMIC SYSTEMS

All political systems operate within the framework of an economic system. Most of politics is involved in taxing and redistributing wealth. The Founders knew this and considered it a necessary evil but they wanted to limit it. It was for that reason, they put into the Constitution, no personal income tax by government. In 1913, that was changed with the passage of the FED Reserve Act and the 16th Amendment allowing an income Tax. Prior to 1913, the Government's revenues came from taxes on liquor, tobacco and imports (tariffs). Today these taxes represent 3% and the income tax represents 97% of the government's income. This is ideal for transnational companies who are incorporated here but have plants overseas since they keep their profits off shore and the citizens do not. The different economic systems are concerned with who pays the taxes and who gets the taxes. The contrasts are clear when one refers to Exhibit 3.

- The Socialists and Communists are on the Left. All socialist and communist systems have failed over the last 100 years. They have no private property and ideally want to redistribute the wealth evenly to all. This violates the human psyche of self-interest.

- The Centrist Welfare state is on the left (John Maynard Keynes/progressives). This is where the government intercedes and spends money on virtually everything including services such as social security, free medical and other programs rather than relying on the American principle of personal responsibility. This is what is happening today and over the last 70 years and as Margaret Thatcher said, *"Socialism is great until the money runs out."*

- Jurist Naturalists de-facto used Austrian Economics – this is *"laissez nous faire"* economics which means, *"Leave us alone"* referring to the government. The free enterprise industrialists / entrepreneurs believe that if you *"leave us alone"*, we will maximize taxes on imports and duties to the state. This was the American way until 1913.

- In the 30s and 40s, Roosevelt introduced socialist / progressive policies of the government into people's lives with no evidence that it improved life for the people – but it got him reelected. The US was still in a depression in 1940. He used what is now called Keynesian economics and socialist services to inject money into the economy. The Supreme Court said that these laws were anti-constitutional. Therefore, he changed the court. He put *"friendly jurists"* on the Supreme Court because most of his new laws were ruled unconstitutional. The new Supreme Court jurists ruled that these laws were constitutional.

- Today, we have in many instances a socialist - fascist government and very active global forces urging all governments toward the New World Order, which is a Communo-Fascist, form of government.

Finally, it is relevant to note that Socialism, Communism, and Keynesian have now all failed. Austrian economics, the model that fits the founding fathers policies, grew this nation from founding to 1913 now needs to be reconsidered. Why? It worked.

It is relevant to note that the US currently has a bi-modal economy. It has very large transnational companies that this paper refers to as the *"Group"* that control the nation and its policies for their benefit not the citizens. However, the largest numbers of businesses, that employ the most people, are small or medium size. These can and do still operate as Austrian Economics entrepreneurships. The US is at a turning point analogous to Rome in 100 BC. The Republic died (about 50 BC) when the Caesars took over the political running of the empire but the freedom for entrepreneurships was allowed to continue. Thus, the citizens flourished economically even though they lost their political freedom. Essentially, they gave up their political freedom to get the state to leave them alone to make money. This seems to be the model that holds in China and is currently happening in the US. If so, remember that Ben Franklin wisely advised, *"Those that give up freedom for safety loses both."*

PRINCIPLES OF AUSTRIAN ECONOMICS

Austrian Economics differ from Keynesian economics primarily in the lack of government control or regulations in any aspect of the entrepreneur / capitalist's business. Keynesian Economics promotes government planning, regulation and money. All of which lead to less growth, less freedom and less profits. It has taken three generations from the 30s to agree and understand that is has now been proved that the Keynesian theme of more government spending will resuscitate an economy in a recession does not work. The QE1, QE2 and tentative QE3 only help the *"Group"* of bankers that benefitted from the handouts from the treasury - not the citizens. The economy is down; unemployment is up; housing capital is down; the dollar is rising but is on the verge of collapse which will occur after the first of the year when the SDRs become center in world trade; the nation's credit is questioned by the international community as proved by the FED monetizing the debt; small and medium businesses cannot get loans and the recession is getting deeper. Yet the Obama government and the FED have no viable plan to turn things around. QE did not work on QE1, QE 2 or QE3 and will not work if it is tried again. However, the banks will get bigger. This is a clear form of fascism.

The Austrian economic model needs to be imposed to get the country moving again.

This is what is needed:

- Government
  - First, government needs to be out of the picture with little or no intervention. Ideally, it is a "laissez faire" economy.
  - Second, private property must be protected since it is used for investment and that is what drives the economy.
  - Third, all laws should benefit the sovereign nation not the international "Group" of transnationals. American citizens first.
  - Fourth, the country must have a sound money system. Businessmen need a sound money system that can be counted on over time so that they can plan. This means that the FED reserve notes must be removed with a new dollar. Ideally replace the FED notes with a Treasury dollar that is backed by a hard commodity such as gold.

- Private property must be protected. Profits earned from private invested property are the start of economics. Without them, nothing happens.
  - With profits, the entrepreneur invests in new plant and equipment in order to get greater profits.
  - The spending on new plant and equipment creates jobs in the new plant and new jobs when the plant comes online.
  - The new jobs at the new plant create income for the workers.

- Consumption
  - The workers buy goods and services to support their families with their wages.

- Taxes
  - The government taxes the wage earner and the service provider.

- National versus Transnational Manufacturers
    - National: When goods and services are bought from national manufacturers and service providers, they create jobs, income and taxes from the other providers within the Nation. This increases employment, tax revenue and the GDP.
    - Transnational: When these goods and services are bought from manufacturers and service providers outside of this nation; jobs in this nation are lost; income is lost; taxes are lost. The "balance of payments" becomes negative and the GDP for the nation is lessened.

- The Economy: A standard economic equation for GDP holds where $Y = C + I + G + BOP$ (Balance of Payments) where Y is gross domestic product of all goods and services, C is consumption of the people, I is investment which only comes from savings (S) and is also equal to or less than savings, G is government expenditures and BOP is the net money flow of goods and services into and out of the US. There are minor adjustments to GDP that will be ignored here but this provides that fundamental relationships.

- Taxes: Transnational companies that manufacture overseas, ship goods to the US, keep jobs and profits (currently at $2.0 trillion) overseas where they currently are dodging taxes. This also increases the negative flow of BOP and is thus bad for the nation because it costs jobs and tax revenue.

- To increase GDP: One must invest in new plant and equipment in this nation, keep the jobs within the nation, tax the employees and companies within the nation, maximize exports, minimize imports, and support in a reasonable way the defense of the nation.

Think about this. Item by item, all of these are the policies that China is following and the US is not following. They do pick certain industries and invest in them as well as encourage foreign firms to invest. Two are rail and semiconductors. However, most industries are free to invest and grow without any state intervention. We are importing goods from China, exporting our manufacturing (6.3 million manufacturing jobs lost so far), allowing transnational firms to keep profits overseas ($2.0 trillion) where they hire foreign workers (many in China) and invest in new plant and equipment in that country (Intel and Motorola each have $1 billion semiconductor plants in China) rather than investing in the US thereby creating more US debt because the economy and taxes do not support our government socialist policy services spending levels. In short, there is very little that we are doing right per the Austrian economists, it shows with 35 million unemployed representing an unemployment rate of 22.7%, FED debt of $ 20 trillion, and 50 million people currently on food stamps with government announced plans for 60 million.

All economies have business cycles. Government intervention normally creates deeper recessions or higher peaks, which are misplaced capital bubbles. The US is currently at a low point that I will call a depression entered into in 1Q08. The Austrian economic model needs to be followed to get the nation out of this depression. However, the current administration policies are of more debt, more government intervention, more international supra national controls. This approach is going to make the depression deeper and hyperinflation will occur over the next few years. This will in turn cause the economy to collapse, which means stops as it did in Germany in 1923. We need to go back to Capitalism not forward to government-imposed socialism and corporate controlled fascism.

SUMMARY

Exhibits 1, 2 and 3 provide insight into the political spectrum that fits all the political categories that are commonly talked about today. The necessary doctrinal steps required to reach both Communism and Fascism were reviewed, noting that Marx specified that Communism require that Socialism exist first and that Socialism is a transitional state between Capitalism and Communism. It was established that America currently has many elements of both Socialism and Fascism - - - both being centrist state collectivist "isms". The New World Order requires both Communism and Fascism. If the U.S. accepts the New World Order, they will have to act as if they are atheist, give up Constitutional principles associated with war and banking and lose many of their political freedoms. The lesson from history is that all politicians want power and non-elected collective centrist governments give them the most power over the citizens. The European Union is but one example. The EU uses appointed officials in Brussels to manage the EU with superimposed regulations not voted upon by the people nor agreed to by their elected representatives. It is a power trip for the virtually unknown bureaucrats in Brussels but the people are finally revolting. BREXIT happened in the UK and at this point Italy appears to be next.

In conclusion, it appears as if the nation has come a long way from the Juris Naturalists or Libertarian views. However, have we really? It is a matter of fact that the central government politicians have become socialist and fascist in their actions if not beliefs. Many are promoting for a New World Order, possibly not knowing what it means, in their speeches and practices but the population is beginning to say "No" as evidenced by the revolt against Obama Care and the massive rallies that Donald Trump gets when he promotes "drain the swamp" in Washington. The bailout programs of TARP, GM, QE1 and 2, as well as the revolt against increasing the debt limits are further signs of discontent and mismanagement.

The nation is at a crossroads. Should they continue on the current path or consider and alternative? What is that alternative?

CHAPTER 3

QUO VADIS? – LIBERTY, FREEDOM AND POLITICAL LEADERSHIP

QUO VADIS?

Where Is The Nation Today? Where does Liberty and Freedom fit? And, where do we go from here?" America is at a turning point in its history. It is up to American citizens as to what road to travel.

A guest editorial in the Wall Street Journal on March 12, 2011, written by Daniel Hannan, a UK member of the European Parliament, labeled, *"A European's Warning to America"*, provides a timely outsider insight into what America should do, why they should do it and what they should stop. I use this article and will paraphrase rather than direct quote. His editorial was directed against Obama's policies and exposes what Obama is really trying to accomplish. His advice is simple, *"Don't do as Europe has done"*. He advises that the US should not become a socialist and fascist state. He does not mention the New World Order but these are the primary requirements for establishing the NWO. Apparently, Europe has come close to the New World Order and European citizens do not like it. He sees that Obama is not setting a random set of policies in place but rather a clear set of directed policies that would make America like Europe and he believes that this is the wrong strategy for America and the world.

Why does Mr. Hannon take this position? He explains that European citizens now recognize that their policies have been wrong and are now just beginning to try to correct them. He then directly addresses what Obama is doing wrong for America. Specifically, Obama is putting the structure in place for another socialist / fascist Europe. This is the basic structure for the New World Order. He explains why this is wrong for America *and the world* by providing some examples:

- European Health care system – healthcare is a failure in Europe as compared to the United States. Europeans come to the US for the best healthcare.

- European carbon taxes – a failure in Europe in that they are expensive and do nothing to stop a problem that does not exist. I further note that they were rejected in the US but that this taxation provides funds for the NWO to support a global army that is the goal of the NWO.

- European day care – expensive socialism. Hillary Clinton has proposed this in her run for the presidency.

- European state directed college education – the American free enterprise educational system is better as proven by the fact that the American system is the best in the world. When the government starts paying for Junior College as proposed by the Democrats, government controls will start and the education will deteriorate.

- European foreign policy – has been a failure for the last 40 years. Specifically, Europe has engaged supranational technocracies – UN, EU and NATO where you get no vote and must pay taxes. Further, Nuclear disarmament leaves the

EU vulnerable. Finally, a reluctance to deploy forces overseas even when in Europe's interest is shortsighted and wrong. For example Italy, a European member of the EU, is getting about 35% of its oil from Libya; yet they cannot get the EU to forcefully intervene.

WILL AMERICA CONTINUE AS A SUPER POWER?

Daniel Hannon's conclusion is that if America continues doing these things, it will no longer be a super power. Why? He explains that America's political Institutions will gradually evolve from those of our founders that put limited power in the state to become like those in Europe where the nations now have institutions that no longer represent the people and where freedom is gone. He provides the following examples -

- The European Union (EU) places supreme power in the hands of 27 unelected Commissioners invulnerable to public opinion.

- Referendums from the people as in Ireland, France, and Netherlands that said that they did not want to join the EU are simply ignored and thrown aside.

- The financials of the EU have not been audited in 12 years and no one does anything about it. Christopher Story reported on this fact in the last 4 years before his death.

- The EU ruling *"document"* clearly establishes that the nation state must be transcended. This means that the world will be organized and managed by regions. This doctrine, by itself, is extremely important because it sets forth and enforces the policy that *"freedom"*, *"democracy"* or the *"rule of law (natural law)*"for the individual is no longer valid. *<u>The state interest is always more important than individual freedom and it is now written into black letter law</u>*.

- One of the worst aspects of the current European system is the impact on the economy. Europe grew dramatically after W WII because of help from the US with their Marshall Plan that funded growth needed to meet the pent up demand. That demand has been fulfilled and the help has ceased. The socialist governments placed in power during this period have burdened the state with socialist policies, bureaucracy, more spending and higher taxes that resulted in slower growth such that the individual is and has been worse off in Europe compared to his American counterpart over this period.

  The net result of the socialist driven economy is that Europe has fallen further behind the Americans in the last 40 years as evidenced by its lower standard of living and the creation of a higher level of structural unemployment than in the US. The US unemployment at 22.5% is less than that in Europe.

He concludes that the US should not follow Europe. They should stop the US progress toward a socialist state. This means that they should avoid going down the path Obama has set for the Europeanization of America. He points out that the US is a repository of our (British) traditional freedoms, which include common Law, based on Natural Law, the Magna Charta (1215) and England's Bill of Rights (1689). He believes that these individual freedoms for the citizens are dying in the UK.

He explains that the EU has already surrendered a large part of the individual's birthright of freedom. The Europeans biggest fear is that Americans have forgotten their birthrights of freedom and liberty embedded in their Constitution and Common Law. He says that In the US today, government to fund bailouts and nationalizations with no effort to get approval by means of Constitutional or Congressional consent is commandeering colossal sums ($6 trillion so far).

He is right since these actions were done with Executive orders whose questionable Constitutional basis is ignored by Congress and remains non-tested by the Supreme Court. Thus, the US is falling into a trap and is making the same mistakes that Britain has in their past by:

- Ignoring its constitution;
- Expanding its government;
- Regulating private commerce;
- Centralization by the state of its jurisdiction in all areas of life;
- Breaking the link between taxation and representation; and
- In the end abandoning its sovereignty.

America just elected Donald Trump who is closely tied to Wall Street banking and has been a very successful entrepreneur. He has proposed a first 100 day plan to turn this nation around. Many of the items directly address the concerns above. The only question should be – Will he meet his objectives? Historically, he has been successful and the world is watching him.

Nonetheless, this is quite an indictment. Given that he says that the US is the depository of English Freedoms, let us examine the concept of liberty and freedom from this nation's history and tradition to better understand what Daniel Hannon means.

AMERICA'S HISTORY OF INDIVIDUAL FREEDOM IN NATURAL LAW

America today is at a crossroad. Do we want to give up our freedoms, the constitution, the Bill of Rights and our heritage of morally directed citizen government for the UN or any institution at the cost of our sovereignty by continuing down the Obama path? If not, then we must get involved to direct our representatives in government to stop this movement. Imagine a government that is dedicated to the people, run by a Congress and Executive who have uncompromising integrity to do the right thing for the American citizen; that gives no quarter with special interests; that makes no excuses; tells the truth to the American people; and provides the people with no excesses of debt or entitlement programs while providing for our common defense. Unbelievably, this type of government used to exist.

It is instructive to briefly examine how Americans gained our individual freedoms, where they came from and then examine what must be done to get them back. This quest leads us to the nexus of religion and the state. America was founded by Christians initially to guarantee their individual religious freedom and to have economic freedom from state control. They had to leave Europe in order to have religious freedom. This is important to recall. For instance, before the advent of Christianity, separate religious and political organizations were not clearly defined in most civilizations. People worshipped the gods of the particular state in which they lived. Religion, in such cases, was but a department of the state. Today, we see how this type of state is run in Iran and many Muslim countries. Christians introduced the concept of the secular and the spiritual and the concept was based on the words of Jesus: ***"Render to Caesar the things that are Caesar's, and to God the things that are God's" (Mark 12:17).*** Two distinct areas of human life and activity had to be distinguished and a theory of how to accommodate the two powers within the state came to form the basis of Christian thought and teaching from the earliest times.

During the 1st century AD, the Apostles living under a pagan empire, taught respect for and obedience to the governing powers so long as such obedience did not violate the higher, or divine law that was defined as Natural Law because Natural Law superseded political jurisdiction. Divine law was taught as being above secular law from the time of the Greek Sophocles play, Antigone (406 BC). This play had been used as a teaching example in Greece and Rome for 500 years. Antigone was the woman who buried her brother in spite of the King's ruling that he as an enemy combatant was to rot on the field of battle. She argued that there was a higher natural law (Zeus) than the King's law, which said that he was to be buried. During Roman times, they changed the God to Jupiter but maintained the principle. The King put her to death by locking her in a cave but her actions was retold and taught for 500 years that she was right.

The transition came in 325 AD (Constantine 306-337 AD) when the Emperor Constantine declared that henceforth Christianity was the official national Roman religion. Natural Law governed by Jesus was relatively easy for Roman Christians to accept since the concept of Natural Law was written into Roman black letter law with Jupiter as God. They substituted Jesus for Jupiter and then the emperor Constantine made it official. For the Church fathers, who lived in the period when Christianity had become the religion of the Roman Empire, the emphasis on the primacy of the spiritual was strong. The message of Jesus was that of inner freedom and autonomy of the soul – to the exclusion of political concerns. This was enough for 1,500 years. The Church fathers insisted upon the independence of the Church from the state and the right of the Church to judge the actions of the secular ruler. Constantine codified this concept of Natural Law into Roman law during his reign. The Roman God had been Jupiter and was now replaced by Jesus but God's laws could supersede all statute law. With the decline of the Roman Empire, in the fifth century in the West, civil authority fell into the hands of the only educated class that remained—the churchmen. Therefore, the church, which formed the only organized institution, became the seat of temporal as well as spiritual power. This lasted for almost 1,000 years.

In 800, under Charlemagne, the Holy Roman Empire was restored in the West, and by the 10th century, many secular rulers held power throughout Europe in the form of regions under their control. A period of political manipulation of the church hierarchy and a decline in clerical zeal and piety followed where for centuries a struggle of emperors and kings with the popes took place. The conflict was over authority of position of the state versus the Church. During the 12th and 13th centuries, papal power greatly increased.

The medieval struggle between secular and religious power came to a climax in the 14th century with the rise of nationalism and the increased prominence of royalist and canon lawyers. The King wanted control and wanted to take the control form the Roman church. Numerous theorists contributed to the atmosphere of controversy until the papacy finally met with disaster, first in the removal of the popes to Avignon (1309 -1378) under French influence and second with the Great Schism (1378-1415) associated with the effort to bring the popes back to Rome. Church discipline was relaxed and Church prestige fell in all parts of Europe.

In later centuries, the Church was questioned about its religious practices, which were Church created rather than biblical. This culminated with Luther (1484-1546) and the 16th century Protestant Reformation. Virtually all the early settlements in America were Protestant reformation believers. The exception was New Mexico and Florida, which were settled by Spanish Catholics. Both Protestants and Catholics, being Christian, firmly believed in Natural Law with Jesus as the God and the supremacy of their individual religious beliefs over any black statute law.

For the people, this tradition and belief that God's laws supersede black letter law continues to this day as evidenced by the history of Thoreau (1817-1862) and his book, **_Civil Disobedience_** who based his belief that Civil Disobedience was justified if the statute law was wrong as measured by God's law. The Judges at Nuremberg used the same reasoning by declaring Physicians putting 282,000 people to death per black letter statute law was wrong when measured against

God's law when They ruled that these actions were "crimes against humanity". Martin Luther King (1929 – 1968) read Thoreau and got his idea of civil disobedience from that book. He believed that a law in conflict with Natural Law beliefs should not be obeyed. Accordingly, he said that segregation laws were not valid laws. Finally, Gandhi (1869-1948) also read and followed Thoreau and took his ideas to India where it became the basis for his passive disobedience of the UK laws. Martin Luther King said,

> *"A just law is a man-made code that squares with the moral law or the law of God. An unjust law is a code that is out of harmony with moral law. We must not obey an unjust law."*

This is the concept of Natural Law as stated by Thoreau where Martin Luther King as well as Gandhi first studied it. Thoreau got his ideas from Sophocles and over two millennium of tradition and teachings. There are such things as bad civil laws and when that occurs, one has a responsibility and obligation to disobey the state if it violates God's laws. The doctrines of Christian morality based on Natural Law are above statute law. In America, one equates Natural Law with the Judeao Christian ethical teachings. Absolutes exist in these teachings in sharp contrast to relative morality that exists in the popular press and in Fascist beliefs.

Liberty

Daniel Hannan expresses his fear that Americans have forgotten their birthrights of freedom and liberty embedded in their Constitution as well as Common Law based on Natural Law. Let us examine this fear to determine whether this is true. First, we will review the concept of liberty and its history. For our purposes, there are two categories of liberty relevant here. First, one has National Liberty that consists of political liberty - - - the national independence and autonomy of a people to govern themselves under laws they give themselves. Then we have Individual Liberty that consists of the freedom of the individual to live as he or she chooses as long as he or she does not infringe on the freedom of another individual.

The concept of liberty came from the Greeks and was later embedded in Roman law from which the Christian philosophers in the middle ages took it up. Liberty was based on Natural Law where all men are created free and equal. However, the Roman emperors to be the giver of this Natural Law established the "Divine rights of Kings". This meant that the King could override the Natural Law. This is pure conflict with the secular and the Church that represented the moral. In Rome, it was believed that all men were created equal and endowed by their creator with the inalienable right of liberty and that governments derive their just power from the divine rights of kings - - - not from the consent of the governed. In addition, although Natural Law was above Roman constitutional Law, it was believed that the Roman Emperor could legislate their beliefs any way they desired. Roman constitutional black letter law provided the following rights:

- To vote and participate in politics;
- To have equality of an individual under the law;
- To have freedom from arbitrary arrest;
- To have the right to trial by jury;
- To have freedom of speech;
- To have economic freedom;
- To have freedom to worship but only the Roman Gods since this, along with Latin, were the unifying themes of the state; and
- To have an ordered liberty within the framework of the Roman constitution.

John Locke (Libertarian)

It was the philosophy of John Locke (1632 – 1704) that greatly influenced the founders. He first proposed that an individual had the right to "life, liberty and property" and this was provided by our creator in Natural Law and not a King. Jefferson's first draft of the Declaration of Independence included the word, *"property"* but the other founders changed this to *"life, liberty and the pursuit of happiness"*. Note that they kept the part of *"provided by our creator"*.

Locke believed that the right to liberty justified the overthrow of government if necessary to obtain those rights. He based this view on Natural law and the long history of England's fight for liberty -

- Magna Charta (1215) where trial by jury and Habeas Corpus was guaranteed;
- Petition of Rights (1628) where habeas corpus, no billeting of troops and no martial law in times of peace was specified
- England's Bill of Rights (1689) where the right to bear arms and freedom of speech was guaranteed.
- By the time of George III, there was a general belief among Colonists that Natural Law or God's laws superseded secular law.

This created a belief system for liberty that existed at the time of America's Declaration of Independence.

- That that government is under Natural Law – not above;
- That secular government rests on the consent of the governed - not a king;
- That a representative government was necessary for the people; and
- Per Locke, the right to revolution was justified by Natural Law.

This discourse on Christian principles in the West led to America and the French Revolution and in the East to the Russian revolution since they did not follow the same line of Natural Law philosophy but continued in the Roman law where the head of state can override the law.

American Liberty Documents

America's Constitution was based on a set of principles specified clearly in the Declaration of Independence. Since America has the only constitution in the history of the world that was based on a set of principles, let us examine them. The four principles of the Declaration are clearly stated and they are:

- The right to self-determination;
- Government is by consent of the governed and government are instituted to secure the citizen's natural rights;
- The right of revolution; and
- The right of being governed by Natural Law not the will of a secular law and a single man and where God is the author of Natural Law not the head of state One notes that *"God"* is used 4 times in the Declaration).

The constitution was written to meet these principles and Daniel Webster said of that document, **"Miracles do not cluster. Hold on to the Constitution of the United States."** The constitution was conceived, written and formed by a unique set of statesmen who had an intense education in freedom; the history of freedom; the classics of Greece and Rome; and they were educated to think historically. Thus, the Constitution was shaped by the legacy of Greece, Rome, England and colonial America as well as thinkers like Locke and Montesquieu. The founders knew certain absolutes from their study of history from Greece and Rome; these were that *"power corrupts"* and *"democracy leads to tyranny"*.

The founders were avid students of Polybius (200-118BC) who was a Greek Historian of the Hellenistic period and was noted for his work, *The Histories*, which covered the period 264 – 146 BC. The work describes the rise of the Roman Republic to its dominance of the Mediterranean world and included an eyewitness account of the sack of Carthage in 146 BC. He was important since he was the first that wrote about a mixed constitution with separation of powers in government. This influenced Montesquieu's work, *The Spirit of the Laws,* which was read and used by the framers of the US Constitution.

Because of their studies, the founders followed the Roman rather than Greece constitution as a model. Polybius had a number of ideas that they followed including the balanced Constitution of Rome and the three elements of the Roman Constitution:

- The Executive was modeled on Roman Counsels;
- The House of Representatives was based on the democracy of the Roman assemblies;
- The Senate was modeled on the Roman Senate with a guiding small group of exceptionally capable individuals. The Senate was to be elected and appointed by state legislatures – the leaders in each colony
- The founders studied Montesquieu who believed that a Judiciary had to be independent and the English American constitution was the only one in the world where political liberty was the direct goal of the Constitution.
- Finally, the founders upon pressure from the colonies took parts of the Bill of Rights from the state constitutions.

It is relevant to note that the Constitution left two open questions that were resolved by the Civil War. One was slavery and the other was where do my loyalties lie - - - with the state or the nation? Lincoln addressed both of these issues in his Gettysburg address, which is significant founding document.

The Fall of The Roman Empire

It is relevant here to point out what caused the Fall of Rome. America has an empire. We have military in 135 nations. We support and defend the free world. This provided a safety net for the free world. Gibbons, in his book, *The Decline and fall of the Roman Empire*, lists the following as the cause:

- Restrictions on individual freedoms
- Increased military spending
- Enormous and ineffective bureaucracy
- Increasing burden of taxation that destroyed the middle class.

All of these things are applicable to the current US economy. We are on the edge of failure but Trump's programs can turn the situation around.

Politician vs Statesman

Lincoln was a statesman, which is more than a politician. We have only a few statesmen today among all of our politicians. What is the difference? History has shown that a statesman possesses the following four qualities:

- A bedrock of principles;
- A moral compass;
- A vision for his country; and
- The ability to achieve a consensus to accomplish the vision.

Lincoln was probably America's most religious president whose Gettysburg address has the feel of a religious sermon with stirring language. He used terms of birth and rebirth to make an analogy to Christ. He used the analogy of Christians dying and rebirth from sin and the nation being reborn this time to purge slavery. He believed in rebirth that will ensure that *"liberty will not perish from this earth"*.

Lincoln created a nexus of morality and God as the foundation of American democracy. As such, the Gettysburg address has become on par with the Declaration of Independence as a document of principles for America.

In the 20th century, there were a few great statesmen. Often mentioned are FDR and Churchill. FDR was a liberal progressive whose principles are part of Keynesian socialism. He introduced and made standard a large, powerful, costly and bureaucratic intrusive federal government that was paid for with IRS taxation. This is a centrist socialist approach where the central government is in control and individual liberty is suppressed. His programs kept him in office for four terms. He had a vision but it was not for individual freedom. It was for state centrist control.

Churchill was a statesman who believed in and fought for political liberty, individual liberty and economic liberty. Lord Acton (1834-1902) studied and identified liberty from its origin in Greece and the great political leaders in history. He found that true liberty exists when:

- Every individual is free to follow his conscience;
- The individual is more important than the majority;
- Government rests on the consent of the governed;
- Government has the duty to encourage the social welfare in education, social welfare and retirement;
- The citizens have a duty to overthrow an unjust and immoral government; and
- Morality was more important than politics. He found that absolute moral values do and must exist to guarantee freedom. To attain liberty, a nation and its leaders must chart the nation's course by the absolute values of morality.

Lord Acton found two types of enemies of liberty. He believed that Darwinism and racism were enemies but that the greatest enemies of liberty were Nationalism and Socialism.

LIBERTY IN TODAY'S WORLD

Finally, where does this leave us today? There are five major dimensions of freedom – each represents an opportunity and potential threat. The balance must be maintained by our political leaders - - - ideally statesmen. These leaders need to be statesmen in order to discern and lead. Today few politicians would pass the test for statesmen. The founders believed that history was the most useful discipline for the citizens of a free republic because human nature does not change and lessons of the past were the best guide to current decisions and the best guide to chart a course for the future. The five dimensions of freedom are national, individual, economic, scientific and spiritual.

National Freedom

National freedom started at the Greek battle of Marathon (490 BC) that gave birth to the idea of freedom; the battle of Cannae (Punic War – 216 BC) that gave birth to the Roman state; and the American and French revolutions that caused freedom to be the most dynamic force in politics. Individual freedom was the most important freedom of the founders who believed in the freedom to live and choose as long as you did no harm to others. Christianity made a fundamental contribution to individual freedom with Constantine's substitution of Jesus for Jupiter in Natural Law. Christian ideas of liberty were one of the causes that created conflict of state statute law and their beliefs in the slavery issue in the 1850s. Devout Christians in the 1850s believed that slavery was morally wrong and today they believe that abortion and homosexuality are morally wrong. In both of today's instances, the state legislated otherwise and thus conflict arose.

Economic Freedom

Economic freedom was a market economy free from government constraints that was fundamental to Rome and the American founders. Thus, a free market economy was the foundation of Republican Democracy in America and Rome. Today, we would describe this as an Austrian Economic capitalist economy model.

Spiritual Freedom

Spiritual freedom is an inner freedom to follow your own conscience. Examples are Thoreau, Martin Luther King and Gandhi. Christianity provided the idea of freedom from sin. Greece, Rome and Christianity believed in an intimate nexus between liberty and morality. Importantly, Herodotus (first historian) began his history with Candaules (King of Lydia 735-718 BC) which teaches the lesson that there is no separation between public and private morality. Our modern politicians and the press try to dodge this absolute doctrine of 2,500 years of history.

Scientific Freedom

Finally, we have scientific freedom. If we no longer believe in the truth of God, do we as a society, implicitly believe in the truth in Science? The Founders believed that science was an invaluable support of our freedom. However, Science has advanced so far and fast that it has raised issues beyond our founders' considerations. Issues such as abortion, euthanasia, cloning and atomic energy are being left to science rather than having moral discussions and judgments such as - When does life start? - Morality says at conception but the law says at first breath; does an individual have a right to choose death early? - morality says no because that is suicide but the law in some states says when you are sick and no longer want to live.; Should cloning be allowed in humans? - Morality says no because that is playing God but the law allows it; and, When is it justified to use atomic energy in war? – Morality would say whenever a nation's life is threatened. It has a right to use any means possible to protect itself. Secular law tries to control and only allow Nuclear among chosen nation states.

The Supreme Court itself presents a moral issue. Rather than using the legislature elected by the people where such questions can be openly discussed in light of the morality of the community and policies established, we leave certain questions to the Supreme Court of 9 men who cannot possibly understand much less wisely view such societal shaking questions as posed and their answers. We, and Congress have allowed the Supreme Court to extend its jurisdiction into social areas where the founders clearly knew should have been left to the legislature which represent all the people and not to a politically appointed and thereby biased few. We have allowed Roman law to supersede Natural Law and allowed the Emperor to decide.

Revolution?

Thus far, we have reviewed the definitions, doctrines and the lessons from history. Americans seem to have rejected those lessons or are ignorant of them at the public official level and the press level. The press is referred to as *"controlled"* since they often come out with statements and directions that are in direct opposition of Christian beliefs, Natural Law and common sense. For instance, it is stated in the press that a politician's private morality has nothing to do with his ability to lead a nation. This is in direct conflict with 2,500 years of Western history, Natural Law and Christian beliefs.

Americans now seem to believe that it is a politician's right to lie to the citizens. We believe that government can lie, steal property and kill with little or no explanation much less payment for moral wrongs. Yet, we have learned from Western history, from Socrates, Cicero, Lord Acton, John Locke, Gandhi and Martin Luther King there was a nexus between truth and liberty and that absolute truth is fundamental to natural law that was written into the Constitution. The question remains, as a society, if we no longer believe truth is an absolute value, then with that rejection have we also rejected natural law as the basis of our liberty and this nation? If so, we have rejected liberty for our society.

It is apparent that at the individual citizen level, a sense exists across America that something is wrong. The citizens are revolting slowly in the TEA parties, the disbelief in the socialist Obama care legislation and the revulsion toward continuing removal of personal liberties in the Patriot Act, the Military Commission Act of 2006 (enemy combatant) and the John Warner Defense Act as well as the unbridled spending. They must start choosing elected officials that are statesmen not just politicians. We must choose men who show a bedrock of principles for freedom; a moral compass that shows tested character and adherence to moral values; a vision for the country that is for freedom; and who has the ability to achieve a consensus to accomplish his vision. If we cannot find such men and put them into office, then we should at least recognize what John Locke and our founders knew and act when a government exists that is so bad that something must be done.

JOHN LOCKE AND REVOLUTION

John Locke was the political philosopher that was admired by all the founders. Locke defined the requirements that must be met to justify a revolution - a government that substitutes arbitrary will of the executive for Law; a government that limits the legislative power from acting freely; a government that alters the mode of electing the legislative body; and a government that delivers the people into a foreign power. Let us examine these points in light of today's world and recent events:

A Government That Substitutes Arbitrary Will of The Executive for Law

The last four presidents have violated this point. Note that no declaration of war was made in Libya, Iraq or Bosnia; rather it was the will of the executive that got the US these wars. The Obama Czars are not in the Constitution or our heritage. Department heads are to be vetted by Congress. In addition, Executive orders are de-facto law made by the arbitrary will of a single man at the top rather than from the legislature. This is not constitutional. It is Platonism or rule by a King.

A Government That Limits the Legislature Power from Acting Freely

The 2,200 page Obama Care bill was handed to the Congress just hours before they had to vote on it. This certainly limits the legislative power from acting freely. In addition, the Frank / Dodd Financial bill was handled in the same manner. Finally, the $700 billion TARP plan was handled by allowing virtually no time to review and it clearly helped the banks not the citizens.

A Government That Delivers the People into a Foreign Power

American citizens have been put at risk of their lives by placing them under UN control in the actions in Libya, Korea, Bosnia, Iraq and NATO control in Afghanistan by executive order - - - not a Senate vote for War.

A Government that Alters the Mode of Electing the Legislative Body

The President is part of the elected legislative body. Obama claims he is native-born American but may not be and thus was not eligible to run for President. His refusal to be vetted on his birth certificate is at least prima facia evidence that he has *"altered the mode of electing the legislative body"*. Even though he released his "birth certificate" as his proof that he is native born, most believe it is a fraud. Further, the Supreme Court has held that Native Born means that both parents were born in this country. This is not true with Obama.

In summary, the above analysis, based on the rules used by the founders to justify revolution against the King of England, when applied to the US government today arrive at the same conclusion - - - a revolution is justified. Today, the education system in America has been "dumbed down" to the level where history of our founders is almost absent and John Locke is not even mentioned. All mention of Christian moral values and Natural Law has been removed from the state schools teachings. However, our heritage, history and founding public documents clearly show that we are living in times where people should be upset with our government. Usually the best way to change America is within the system using the courts and the voting booths. However, the courts have become politicized and are *"legislating from the bench"* at times.

The current Obama administration has hurt itself by

- Being arbitrary, almost dictatorial in jamming laws through Congress;
- Cutting back on retired Social Security COLA;
- Using the funds from the paid in Medicare advantage programs to pay for illegals' medical care. This removedMedicare Advantage program benefits;
- Not enforcing illegal immigration laws;

- Attacking countries and creating wars without declarations – Libya, Syria, Iraq;
- Bailing out special interest banking with the HARP program with no constitutional basis;
- Putting millions out of work by restraining drilling in the Gulf and north shore;
- Providing no tariffs on goods and services coming into thiscountry that cause jobs to leave;
- Supporting green policies like ethanol that raises prices of food is not efficient but subsidizes a select few donors;
- Supporting unions to keep people from choosing whether they want to be in a union or not;
- Introducing CORE education into the state educational system by extortion – install it or you lose Federal funding.

During a revolution, people are focused on who wants to have the most power. In this case, it is clear that the people will gain power again only by removal of people, money, function, agencies and regulations. This can be done with a political revolution by changing the people in Washington as being proposed in this Clinton / Trump election cycle. Trump is right, *"We must drain the swamp."*

CONCLUSION

All Americans should be dedicated to get the country back to the Constitution, Common Law, Natural Law, juris naturalist policies, limited centrist government and providing more function at the state level and less at the central level. The Federal government has become too large and has extended its jurisdiction into areas that belong to the states. Our freedom depends on slimming down the government and putting function like education back into the states. Return to these principles will go a long way to right the ship of state. Our education system needs to be revised to bring back the Christian principles that were embedded in the people and made this nation different from all others on earth. This can only be done if parents are involved. They have been removed. Natural Law needs to be explained in relation to American history and the foundational documents of this nation. These principles of morality that were accepted and followed by the ordinary citizen is what won the hearts, souls and loyalty of the immigrants that came to this country up to recent years.

The power of the Supreme Court to legislate their ideas in social matters that are not based on doctrines specified in the Constitution but rather on principles and doctrines that they create needs to be revised, limited and in some cases reversed. This has been done in the past and can be done again by Congress by legislation that says that certain areas of social matters are out of your jurisdiction. If the Supreme Court says that the new law is unconstitutional and that the Congress cannot rule certain areas are out of our jurisdiction, then the Congress and the Executive should reply as Andrew Jackson did by asking, "Where is your army?" - - - and ignore them. It was he who said, **"One man with courage makes a majority".**

Finally, this was written to inform and review our history of natural law, economics, liberty, political affiliations, economic systems and current new world order goals. If it did its job, the reader will now have enough information to get involved with your Congressman and TEA parties and let them know what you think. Today the Nation is in trouble economically and politically with a very weak Congress, President and Supreme Court that have all been influenced by the New World Order "Group". Most have been in office too long and as Lord Acton said, **"Power corrupts."** America just elected an outsider as the president. Donald Trump understands finance and how to build. I have reviewed his first 100-day plan. If implemented, it will be a great start on turning this ship of state around and making American great again.

Part II will concern the current economy and an action plan that if followed would enable the new political leadership to get the nation back to the constitution, capitalism, natural law, the economy booming to put 15 million people back to work and getting 44 million people off of food stamps.

APPENDIX A - TEST

ARE YOU A LIBERAL? LIBERTARIAN? or CONSERVATIVE?

The idea for this appendix comes directly from David Boaz's outstanding book, **_The Libertarian Mind._** He also creates an appendix that asks this question. I do not use his questions but use similar questions. I redrew his matrix and extended the concept to include calculations to determine given that an individual scores A on the Personal Freedom category and B on the Economic category, he can determine what percentage he scores on a Libertarian category. Thus, you can value yourself as a Liberal with Personal score A and Conservative with Economic score B and finally look up on the tables provided to determine your score on a Libertarian scale

The sociological questionnaire concept technique that David Boaz uses is basic and correct so that I am going to reuse it here. I do not use his questions. However, I have modified all the questions to get similar results. The technique of using questions to place yourself on a scale is a sociological tool that has been used for over 60 years and has been found to measure what users believe.

I found that positioning yourself on the scales of Liberal, Libertarian, and Conservative helps orient one's thinking. It is revealing about oneself in that only after the fact does one realize the differences and the end results may conflict with the person's preconceived notions of where he stands. In my case, I thought that I was conservative and found that I am libertarian. It may come as a surprise that most Americans may fall quite high on a Libertarian scale – even those who considered themselves Liberal or Conservative.

Individual Rights

Libertarians start with a simple belief in individual rights. The fundamental question that an individual must face in life is - - - Do you make the decisions that are important in your life, or does someone else like the government make them for you?Libertarians believe that the individual has both the right and the responsibility to make his own decisions.Non-libertarians often believe that the government should make some or many of the important decisions in one's individual life.

As an example, consider the following and decide whether you agree or disagree.

Personal Freedoms

As long as I respect the rights of others, I should have the right to - -

- Read whatever I want – even it offends the beliefs of others in my community.
- Choose the safety equipment that I think is best, even if it is risky.
- Choose the medical treatment that I think is best, even if It's risky
- Choose to not buy insurance even if the government says that I should

In essence, the individual has the freedom of choosing actions over his or her own life. If you agree, then you most likely agree on some basic libertarian positions on libertarian freedoms.

The implication of the above is that the government has no right to establish a religion, enforce any moral codes, regulate pornography, or hate speech. This does not mean that libertarians agree or endorse these positions. Rather, they agree one should havethe right to accept or reject them as their choices.

Economic Freedoms

As long as I am honest with others, I should have the right to earn more money than others and to leave my money to my children even though other children may get less. The individual has the right to make decisions about the results of his labor.

If you agree, then you agree with the Libertarian view of economic freedom.

Government Responsibility

If you believe that the government has the obligation and responsibility to protect an individual's right to life, liberty and the pursuit of property and happiness, then you should be able to measure your libertarianism.

The following questionnaire asks whether you think it should be the individual's decision or the government's decision in the activities divided into *"Personal Freedoms"* and *"Economic Freedoms"*.

Give yourself 10 points if you think that you should decide, 5 points if you are not sure, and 0 points if you think the Government should decide.

Personal Freedoms

Who should decide whether you - - -

Wear a safety helmet while driving a 3 –wheeler or skiing? _____

Own a weapon such as a rifle or hand gun? _____

Do government service by serving in the military or other administration? _____

Use recreationaldrugs that may be illegal? _____

Use medical treatments that have risk? _____

Engage in sexual relationships outside of marriage? _____

Watch pornography? _____

Buy a controversial book that promotes a single gender? _____

Send your child to a school different than the public school assigned? _____

Have access to the Internet without government permission or monitors? _____

Total Personal Freedom Score

Economic Freedoms

Who should decide whether you _____

Buy a foreign vacation or medicine from aforeign vendor? _____

Put retirement savings into private savings rather than Social Security? _____

Give money to charity? _____

Start a barbershop without a license? _____

Hire a worker of a specific religion? _____

Build an addition to a home without a permit? _____

Pay subsidies to ethanolcorn or sugar producers? _____

Work for less than the minimum wage? _____

Set up a company to compete with the US government services such as package delivery Mail? _____

Purchase house insurance? _____

Total Economic Freedom Score _____

Next, look at the matrix in Exhibit 1, Liberal, Libertarian, and Conservative Measurement Scale. The purpose is to fit your beliefs on the scale to reduce the confusion that you may have. These scales provide you some insight as to how coercive and pervasive our government has become in all aspects of our lives.

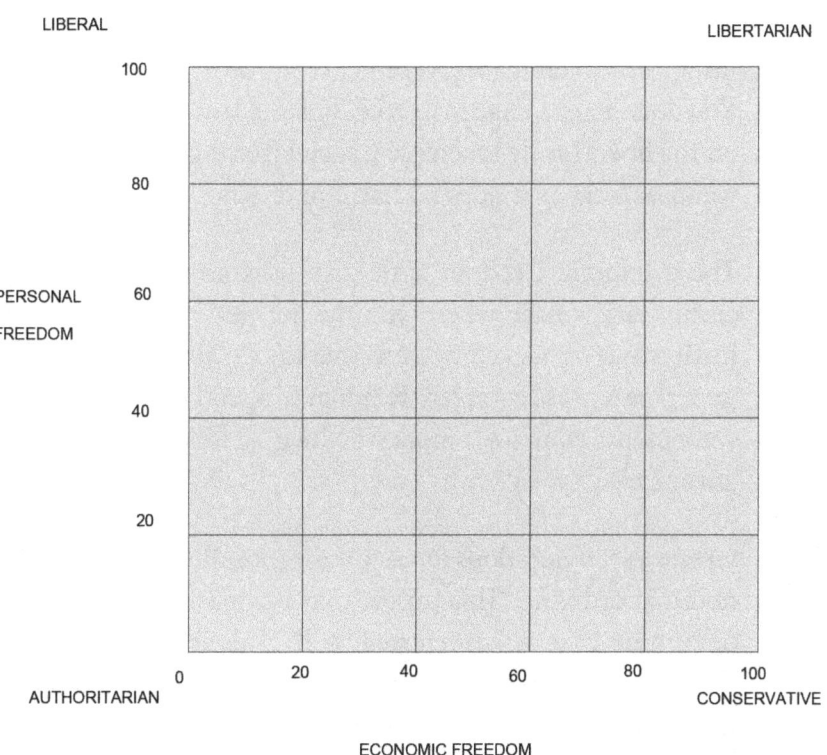

EXHIBIT 3, LIBERAL, LIBERTARIAN, CONSERVATIVE MEASUREMENT SCALE

Subjective Scale Measures

The sociologists have derived a way that allows them to measure attitudes and beliefs. The method is their version of science. It does not use voltmeters or ohmmeters. Rather it uses preferences and then does a lexicographic nominal ordering of those preferences. This is how it works –

1. Choose the topic to be measured. In this instance, it is Liberalism as measured by Personal freedom and Conservatism as measured by Economic freedom. .

2. Choose the extreme points on the measurement scale. In this instance, it is complete government control or authoritarianism. You do not get a chance to vote. It is the law. The upper point on the liberal scale is complete social freedom to do what one wants as long as it does no harm to others.

   The economic freedom scale also uses government as the authoritarian base where you do not get a vote. The state institutes laws backed by guns that says – "do it!" or else. The upper extreme is complete freedom to spend on whatever one wants with your own money as long as it does no harm to anyone else.

3. Create a set if questions for each scale that allows lexicographic nominal ordering. This means that I can ask a question and determine that A is preferred to B. This is usually written A>B. Thus, the questions about personal freedom or economic freedoms imply that the answer is either in favor of or against government control.

4. Create an average of the questions. The way to do this is how David Boaz did. You ask the reader to take the test, record his answers on a personal relative scale from 0 to 10 with a 5 if you are not sure.

5. The two sets of questions provide two answers which lend themselves to an orthogonal plot of X and Y. I have chosen X as Economic Freedom (conservatism) and Y as Personal Freedom (liberalism).

6. Plot the results on the scale as shown. Note that the Libertarian is for both Economic and Personal freedom so it goes in the right upper corner as shown.

If the questions are chosen correctly and you are honestly with yourself, you can see where you stand as a Liberal or as a Conservative. Also, you can see approximately where you fall as a Libertarian. In the next section, we will derive a numerical answer where you stand as a libertarian.

Now that you have your scores, we are just beginning. Consider your Personal Freedom score as a measure of you as a Liberal. Also, consider your Economic Freedom score as a measure of you as a Conservative. AlthoughExhibit 1, Liberal, Libertarian, Conservative Measurement Scale, gives the reader some feel where he fits on the Libertarian Scale, we can improve that measure. We are going togive you a more precise feel as to how "Libertarian" you are.

Libertarian Scale

The following two tables provide an analysis that allows you to fit yourself on the Libertarian scale that is a diagonal from zero to 100 on the upper right corner.

First, consider any point on Exhibit 1. Let us say 60 points conservative and 80 points liberal. This represents two rectangles, one that is 60x60 both liberal and conservative which is the libertarian box since it is 50% each - - - and one that is the total measure of 60x80 total. The areas of the libertarian divided by the total gives 75% for a score of libertarian. Using this reasoning, Table 1, Questionaire, Libertarian Percentage Calculations, shows all the points and calculations for determining the Libertarian percentage for any two X-Y coordinates. For instance, the example of 60 for conservative and 80 for liberal provides the result 75% for libertarian. It also shows how it is calculated.

QUESTIONAIRE_LIBERTARIAN PERCENTAGE CALCULATIONS

	Conservative Area	Libertarian Area	Total	Conservative Area	Libertarian Area	Total	Conservative Area	Libertarian Area	Total	Conservative Area	Libertarian Area	Total	Conservative Area	Libertarian Area	Total
Y-Axis Personal															
20	20	400	400	40	800	1600	60	1200	3600	80	1600	6400	100	2000	10000
Libertarian %			100%			50%			33%			25%			20%
40	20	800	1600	40	1600	1600	60	2400	3600	80	3200	6400	100	4000	10000
Libertarian %			50%			100%			67%			50%			40%
60	20	1200	3600	40	2400	3600	60	3600	3600	80	4800	6400	100	6000	10000
Libertarian %			33%			67%			100%			75%			60%
80	20	1600	6400	40	3200	6400	60	4800	6400	80	6400	6400	100	8000	10000
Libertarian %			25%			50%			75%			100%			80%
100	20	2000	10000	40	4000	10000	60	6000	10000	80	8000	10000	100	10000	10000
Libertarian %			20%			40%			60%			80%			100%
	Economic X			Economic X			Economic X			Economic X			Economic X		
X-Axis	20			40			60			80			100		

TABLE 1, LIBERTARIAN PERCENTAGE CALCULATIONS

Find yourself on the X and Y axis and the table calculates the Z Libertarian axis.

Table 2, Percent Libertarian Calculation Results, provides a summary of Table 1 that is easy to use and provides results at a glance. Thus 60 on the conservative X-axis and 80 on the liberal Y-axis instantly provides 75 for the Libertarian scale.

	PERCENT LIBERTARIAN CALCULATION RESULTS				
Y-AXIS (Personal)					
20	100	50	35	25	20
40	50	100	67	50	40
60	33	67	100	75	60
80	25	50	75	100	80
100	20	40	60	80	100
	X	X	X	X	X
	20	40	60	80	100
	X-AXIS (Economic)				
Questionaire Results Were in Two Categories - Personal and Economic					
Results of Table 1 Calculations for % Libertarian are Shown in this Table					

TABLE 2, PERCENT LIBERTARIAN CALCULATION RESULTS

BIBLIOGRAPHY

- *Are you Liberal? Conservative? or Confused?* Richard J. Maybury. Blue Stocking Press, Placerville, California.
- *Charles de Secondat, Baron Montesquieu*, translated by Thomas Nugent, Bell and Sons, London, 1914.
- *Conspirators Hierarchy, The Story of the Committee of 300*, John Coleman, Amazon.com, 1997.
- *Communist Manifesto*, Karl Marx and Frederick Engels, International Publishers, 2014.
- *Creature from Jekyll Island, a Second Look at the Federal Reserve*, G. Edward Griffin, Amazon. Com, 1998.
- *Das Kapital, Karl Marx*. First Rate Publishers, 2014.
- *Declaration of Independence and the Constitution of the United States*, Cato Institute, 1998
- *Federalist Papers* by Hamilton, Madison, NJ, published by Penguin group, NY.
- *Mein Kampf*, Adolf Hitler, 1923
- *Psychological Warfare and the New World Order: The Secret War against the American People*, Servando Ganzalez, Amazon.com, 2010.
- *The History of Freedom and Other Essays*, John Emerich Edward Dalberg, Lord Acton, McMillan, London, 1907.
- *The Histories (220 – 168 BC) 40 volumes*, Polybius.
- *The Histories*, Herodotus, Robert B. Strassler translator, Anchor Books a division of Random House, NY, 2007.

- *The Law*, Frederic Bastiat, Ludwig von Mises Institute, Tribeca Books, 2007
- *The Libertarian Mind, a Manifesto for Freedom*, David Boaz, Simon and Schuster, New York, London, Toronto, Sydney, and New Delhi, 1997.
- *Tragedy and Hope, a History of the World in Our Time*, Carroll Quigley, The McMillan company, New York Collier – McMillan Limited, London, 1966.
- *Two Treatises on Government*, John Locke, Everyman, 1993
- *Wealth of Nations*, Adam Smith, Bantam Classics, 2003
- *Who's Next, Analysis of 66 Mysterious Banker Deaths, Part I: Federal Reserve Banks White Collar Crimes*, Joseph Hawranek, PhD, Trafford Publishing, Edwards Brothers Malloy, Oxnard, CA 2105.
- *Who's Next, Analysis of Fed Plundering in Port Usury (N Y). How Much Booty Is It?, Part II: Fed Reserve Banks White Collar Crimes*, Joseph Hawranek, PhD, Trafford Publishing, Edwards Brothers Malloy, Oxnard, CA 2105.

GLOSSARY

ANARCHIST. Originally, a person who does not believe in political government. Now, it often is used to mean a terrorist.

AUSTRIAN ECONOMICS. This is a free market economic system. The origin was in Vienna, Austria. Austrian economists have won Nobel prizes. S. H. Hayek, was highly influential in the economic policy of the British Prime Minister Margaret Thatcher.. Ron Paul in the United States is a proponent of Austrian economics

CAPITALISM. The term was coined by Karl Marx, who meant the stage of economic development in which capital was accumulated by private firms. Today capitalism is generally taken to mean free market, free trade and free enterprise. It is the economic philosophy of the Libertarians and the right.

CENTRIST. A moderate.

CIVIL LIBERTARIAN. One who believes in the need to protect the individuals rights to free speech, press, religion, assembly, and privacy, but generally not property.

CLASSICAL LIBERAL. Juris naturalist. One who believes that the country should have a small, weak government and free markets and that the individual is endowed by his creator with in the alienable rights to his life, liberty and property. Also, one who believes in natural Law and Common Law or a higher law than black letter law.

COMMUNIST. Originally this was a socialist who was striving to make a utopia of communism in which there is no government and all live according to the rule, "*from each according to his ability, to each according to his needs.*" Now, one who believes in a dictatorial government that owns and controls everything and everyone, including private property.

CONSERVATIV E. A person on the right side of the left right political spectrum conservatives believe in economic freedom and social control.

CONTR ACT LAW. Law of agreements that enables individuals to exchange private property.

COUNTRY. A geographical region controlled by a government.

CRIME. Anything a government punishes.

CRIMINAL LAW. Laws enacted by governments. Criminal law usually are laws against violence, fraud and theft, but in fact, governments can and do criminalize anything they do not like.

DEMOCR AT. A member of the Democratic Party cut. Also, a person on the left side of the political spectrum. They believe in economic control and social freedom.

EMPOWER. To have power or to be granted power over citizens.

ENCROACH. To intrude on, or damage, the life, liberty or property of someone who has not harmed anyone. To trespass.

EXTREMIST. One who is highly committed to a position with which the writer or speaker does not agree.

FANATIC. The same as an extremist.

FASCISM. A political philosophy that is no philosophy at all. One must do what ever appears necessary. It has evolved from the role of law in the Roman empire. The first modern fascist was Mussolini. The Italian government was characterized by large corporations suggesting directions and providing help to politicians. Today, in return for passing laws that aid corporations to make money, the politicians are provided funding for reelection campaigns.

FASCIST. A fascist believes that there is no real truth. He believes that concepts such as justice and right and wrong, or entirely matters of personal opinion. Fascist are generally nationalist who believe in a very strong central government that controls everyone according to a simple rule, "*do what ever appears necessary in order to maintain your position of power.*"

FREEDOM. Permission to do a few pleas within the constraints of laws.

GOVERNMENT. An organization with the legal privilege of encroaching on persons who do not harm anyone.

HIGHER LAW. A law higher than black letter law.

JURIS NATURALIST. Natural law

JURIS NATURALISM. The belief that there is a natural law that determines the results of human conduct, and this law is higher than any government's law.

JURIS NATURALIST. This is synonymous with a classical liberal. One who believes in a higher law or natural law, that right and wrong are not matters of opinion but are absolutes. Believes political power corrupts both morals and judgment. Once a government that is small and not centrist.

KEY NESI ANISM. This is John Maynard Keynes economic philosophy first postured in the 30s. Today it has evolved into a compromise between socialism and capitalism. The objective is to have broad strong central government controls on economic activity and the money supply.

LAISSEZ-FAIRE. This is short for the French, "laissez-nous faire", meaning leave us alone. Government should do nothing in the economy except enforce contracts and protect against violence and theft. Government economic controls are generally less than the total cost.

LAW. The rules for human conduct which are enforced by violence or threats of violence. Sometimes it means Common-law or Natural law is distinct from black letter legislated law. "A nation of laws and not of men." Refers to a nation in which the highest law is Common-law or Natural law or God's law not legislation.

LEFT. The liberal side of the political spectrum.

LIBERAL. A person on the left side of the left / right political spectrum. Liberals believe in social freedom and economic control.

LIBERTARIAN. This is a classical liberal.

LIBERT Y. Liberty is granted by the creator. It is restrained by laws of government. Acting within those laws is freedom. Liberty is fundamental to man's belief that his body, and the result of his work are his property because God gave him the liberty of creating that property with his own labor.

MARXISM. The theory of Karl Marx that human society developed through stages ending in what is called Communism. It was a utopia, which required no laws because it believed in the principle "to each according to his need".

MODERATE. One who is in the middle of the left right political spectrum. Moderates advocate both economic encroachment and social encroachment.

NATIONALIST. An extremely patriotic person who regards his nation as being supreme

NATURAL LAW. These are the laws that govern the universe and everything and everyone in it. Natural law has been considered God's Law by many for millenniums. Further, is is believed that God gave man reason in order to understand and detect what are his laws.

NAZI. A member of the Nationalist Socialist German workers party. This is a fascist. As such, private corporations aided the German government in its objectives, and in turn garnered contracts to forward the government's objectives. These contracts earned the German Corporation much profit.

POLITICAL POWER. The legal privilege of encroaching on the life, liberty or property of a person who has not harmed anyone.

POPULIST. One who is not a Democrat or a Republican, but claims to be popular with the citizens.

RADICAL. Same as an extremist.

REPUBLICAN. Generally on the right side of the political spectrum, but not at the edge. He is considered conservative

RIGHT. The conservative side of the political spectrum.

Serfdom. Economic slavery developed through very heavy taxation.

SIN. The breaking of a moral or religious law.

SOCIALISM. Usually refers to the teachings of Karl Marx and is called Marxism. It is characterized by the government owning all the factors of production.

SOCIALISM – RUSSIAN. Russia used Marxism to create a communist system. It is characterized by state ownership and control of all factors of production. It failed and is being converted to capitalism.

SOCIALISM – DEMOCRATIC SOCIALISM OF GERMANY. The German socialism allows private ownership of all factors of production and private control of production and manufacturing. However, profits must be distributed in the percentages defined by the state. This includes retained earnings, dividends, percent invested in capital and taxes.

SOCIALISM – CONSERVATIVE. This socialism appears in Europe in France and Italy. It is deference to the former nobility. They want to maintain the capitalist system. Therefore, they introduce price and behavior controls to slow the process tor conversion to socialism that is sweeping Europe.

SOCIALIST. A person who advocate socialism. One who assumes government agencies will act in the best interest of the governed, not in the best interests of the government or the bureaucrats that run the government.

SOCIALIZED. Owned and controlled by the government

STATE. Government. Sometimes it means the combination of the government and the country as a single entity.

STATISM. Government is our friend, our protector, the solution to our problems, and there is no law higher than the government's law. This is in sharp contrast to the original American philosophy where the individual believes in higher law in the form of natural law and the individual's belief in a God could overrule black letter government law. The two types of government are in strong conflict. In statism the government is supreme and in the American constitution the individual is supreme.

TERRORISM. Terrorism is usually created through violence or threats of violence. Terrorists could have a just cause or not have one.

TERRORIST. One who creates terror, usually through violence or threats of violence.

TORT. Harm done to another. Encroachment on the life, liberty or property of a person who is not harmed anyone.

TORT LAW. The branch of Common Law dealing with harm one person does to another.

WEALTH. Goods, services and money

WELFARE SYSTEM. The belief that government is responsible for the citizens. It should ensure a minimum standard of living. – Food, clothing, shelter, medical care and schooling. It requires heavy taxes and a large bureaucracy to finance and administer any welfare system. It is the most popular leftist economic philosophy.

ABOUT JOSEPH P HAWRANEK

Joe, also known as "Joe Raven", is a former corporate executive in multiple high-tech computer and communications companies. He retired from IBM as a Global Services certified Communications, Security, and Resiliency (backup) consultant. His served as an engineer and a manager bringing many new products to market. He worked on the Minuteman missile and the Saturn V moon rocket that put a man on the moon. He was also a manager for IBM and brought out their point-of-sale system. At Honeywell he was globally responsible for communications. He developed and shipped the X.25 packet switching system that eventually evolved into the Internet. For 10 years. He ran his own high-tech consulting business that dealt with high-tech companies in technology and financial issues for startups. He consulted with state governments on their phone systems at the university, state government and inmate phones for prisons.

He's been a consultant to firms in the United States and is president of Raven Communications Consulting and Raven Publishing.

He has written six books, two are on the Federal Reserve and the 66 mysterious banker deaths, three are on Hillary Clinton and her 39 years of scandals and corruptions. This six books are focused on the political process in America today and geopolitics.

He has traveled widely in Europe, North and Latin America and in New Zealand.

To date on his site, one can find 140 free articles and 58 articles on his Raven Report which provides geopolitical news from around the world on a weekly basis.

He is a teacher for all ages. His focus in the last eight years has been on geopolitics, which he defines as the study of a nation state in its daily life.

ABOUT RAVEN PUBLISHING

Joseph Hawranek is Pres. of Raven Publishing. He writes an investment and geopolitical newsletter about geopolitics, economics, stocks, bonds, currencies, interest rates, and precious metals. His analysis is based on his formal education in Economics and experience of managing large and small businesses. Mr. Hawranek gives special attention to events in the European Union, the former USSR, and Mideast, China in the East as well as in the United States.

For a sample of the type of work he produces, go to his website and review the index of paid articles. w w w.ravengeopolnews.com

INDEX

A

Adams, John, 20
Adams, Sam, 20, 41,42
American Founders, 21,22,31,32,33,39,40,44,48,54,59,60,61,63, 65,66
Austrian Economics, 63

B

Bible, 20
Bill of Rights, 55,56,59,61

C

Capitalist, 63, 68, 72
Centrist, 62, 67, 75
Common Law, 55, 58, 67, 77, 79
Communism, 4,14,25,28,33,34,36,37,42,49,51,75,77
Conservatives, 78
Constitution,7,11,13,14,17,19,21,24,34,37,39,40,43,44,45,52,56,58, 59,60,61,64,65,66,67,75
Contract, 21, 75
Creator, 19, 22, 59, 75, 77

D

Democratic, 29,32,75,78
Depression, 28,33,48,51
Dialectic, 36
Dictator, 39, 40

E

Economic, 40, 45, 48
Empower, 75
Encroach, 40,77

F

Fanatic, 75
Fascist, 11.12.17, 25, 29, 30,31,32,37, 38, 40, 42, 43, 45.48, 52, 53
Franklin, Benjamin, 6, 20, 49
Free enterprise, 12, 17, 32,33, 36, 48, 53, 75
Freedom, 6,7,8,9,11,14,17,18,21,22,23,27,31,32,37,39,40,43,45,49,5
2, 53,55,56,57,58,59,60,61,62,63,64,65,68,69,70,71,73,75,76,77

G

God, 13,14,18,19,20,21,22,23,25,32,42,43,44,45,56,57,58,59,60,62, 63, 77, 78
Government, 6,7,8,9,10,11,12,13,14,15,17,20,22,23,24,26,28,29,30, 31,33,34,35,38,40,42,45,48,49,50,51,52,53,54,55,5,60,62,63,64, 6566,67,69,70,71
Depression, Great, 28,33,48,51

H

Hamilton, Alexander, 73
Henry, Patrick, 10
Higher Law, 43, 75, 76

Hitler, Adolf, 12, 28, 37, 42, 43, 73

J

Jefferson, Thomas, 20, 59
Juris Naturalist, 18, 20, 22, 23, 40, 41, 52

K

Keynes, John Maynard, 12, 33, 48, 49, 62, 76

L

Laissez Faire, 49, 50
Law,7,8,9,11,13,14,15,18,19,20,21,23,26,30,34,36,37,38,39,42,43,44,45,48,50,54,55,56,57,58,59,60,63,64,65,66,67,68
Left, 6,9,17,25,31,40,48,61,64,75
Legislation, 14,15,16,42,65,67,77
Liberals, 6,7,8,10,11,12,13,17,18,20,23,30,31,33,62,69,71,72
Libertarian, 6,7,8,10,11,12,13,14,17,17,20,40,42,52,59,69,70
Liberty, 6,7,11,14,17,20,22,23,27,40,41,42,43,44,53,55,58,59,60,61,62,63,64,65,66,69
Locke, John, 59,64,65,66,73
Lord Acton, 6,23,62,64,68

M

Madison, James, 20,39
Marx, Karl, 8,11,13,14,16,35,37,42
Mercantilism, 26,27,28,37
Mercantilism, 21st Century, 27
Moderate, 31, 40, 75
Mussolini, 6, 11, 37, 42, 43, 76

N

National religion, 45

NAZI, National Socialist Workers Party, 24, 37, 77
Natural Law, 14,18,19,20,43,44,54,55,56,58,59,60,63,64,66,67,68,75New World Order (NWO), 9,1117,23,24,27,28,29,30,32,40,42,43,44,45,46,48,52,53,67,67,

O

Obamacare, 31
Original American Philosophy, 78

P

Permission, 8, 23, 76
Plato, 23,24,43,65
Political term, 12, 18
Political Power, 22, 23, 37, 76
Political Spectrum, 31, 40, 41, 45, 51, 75, 77, 78

R

Radical, 77
Religion, 19, 20, 21, 23, 45, 56, 57, 70, 75
Republican,12, 29, 31, 63, 77, 78
Revolution, 39,60,63,64
Rights,6,7,8,12,13,14,15,18,20,22,23,24,25,31,32,33,34,38,39,40, 41,42,43,45,55,56,58,59,60,61,64,67,69,71,75,77
Roman Empire, 57,61,76
Russian Socialism, see Socialism, Russian

S

Sin, 22,23,62,78
Smith, Adam, 27,42,73
Social, 6,7,9,15,16,23,31,33,36,40,62,67,75
Socialism, 6,7,8,9,10,11,12,14,15,16,17,24,28,33,36,37,43,44,48,49, 51,52,53,62,76,78

Socialist, 8,10,11,12,16,17,29,30,32,33,37,39,42,45,48,51,52,53,54, 55,62,65,75

State, 6,7,8,9,11,12,13,14,15,16,17,18,19,21,24,27,28,31,32,33, 34, 35,36,37,38,39,40,42,43,44,45,48,51,52,53,54,55,56,57,58,59, 61,62,63,66,67,68

Statism, 22, 33, 78

Socialism, Karl Marx, 12

Socialism, Russian, 15, 85

Socialism, Democratic (Germany), 8, 78

Socialism, Conservative (Italy, France), 15,16

T

Taxation, 16, 53, 55,61,62,78

Tort, 21,22,37,79

W

Welfare statism, 33

i Joseph Hawranek, Ph.D., **W ho's Next? Analysis of 66 Mysterious Banker Deaths, Par t I: Federa l Reser ve Banks W hite Collar Crimes**, Trafford Publishers, North America and International, 2015
Joseph Hawranek, Ph.D., **W ho's Next? Analysis of FED Plundering in Port Usur y (N Y), How Much Boot y Is It? Part II: FED Reser ve Banks W hite Collar Crimes**, Trafford Publishers, North America and International, 2015
ii Servando Gonzales, *Psychological Warfare and the New World Order, The Secret War Against the American People*, Amazon, 2016, https://w w w.amazon.com/Psychological-Warfare-New-World-Order/dp/0932367232
iii Ibid, P.1x
iv John Coleman, *The Committee of 30 0*, 1991, John Coleman was a professional intelligence officer. He relates that he studied and was familiar with Royal Institute of International Affairs (RIIA), Council on Foreign Relations (CFR), the Bilderbergers, the Trilaterals, the Zionists, Freemasonry, Bolshevism-Rosicrucians, and Order of St. John of Jerusalem, German Marshall Fund, the Round Table, the Fabian Society, the Venetian Black Nobility, the Mount Pelerin Society and many others. This study led to his book that he believes rips off the mask of the entire secret upper-level parallel government that runs Britain and the United States.
v Carroll Quigley, *Tragedy and Hope, A History of the World In Our Time*, Macmillan Company, New York, Collier-Macmillan Limited, London, 1966
vi Naomi Wolf, "Fascist America, in 10 Easy Steps", UK Guardian, 24 April 2007

www.ingramcontent.com/pod-product-compliance
Lightning Source LLC
Chambersburg PA
CBHW031157020426
42333CB00013B/704